Stenciling & Embossing GREETING CARDS

18 Quick, Creative, Unique & Easy-to-do Projects

Judith Barker

ABOUT THE AUTHOR

Judith Barker began her stencil business, American Traditional Stencils, in 1979. Her miniature brass templates and laser-cut polyester film stencils are sold worldwide. She is the principle designer in her company, as well as a certified stenciler, teacher and demonstrator. Judy loves teaching and demonstrating and has taught stenciling in several countries. She has produced seven videos, five books and appeared on numerous television programs.

Judy was chosen as New Hampshire's Entrepreneur of the Year in 1997, is frequently published in craft and consumer magazines, and was chosen for Strathmore's *Who's Who in Business*. She is an active member and serves on the boards of several civic and business organizations.

When not involved in stenciling, Judy enjoys the outdoors. Always keeping active, she teaches or participates in various sports and hobbies, including skiing, snowboarding, windsurfing, running, hiking, painting, reading, and enjoying life!

Stenciling & Embossing Greeting Cards. © 2000 by Judith Barker. Manufactured in China. All rights reserved. The patterns in this book are for the personal use of the reader. By permission of the author and publisher, they may be either hand-traced or photocopied to make single copies, but under no circumstances may they be resold or republished. It is permissible for the purchaser to use the designs herein and sell them at fairs, bazaars and craft shows. No other part of this book may be reproduced in any form or by any electronic or mechanical means including information storage and retrieval systems without permission in writing from the publisher, except by a reviewer, who may quote brief passages in a review. Published by North Light Books, an imprint of F&W Publications, Inc., 1507 Dana Avenue, Cincinnati, Ohio 45207. (800) 289-0963. First edition.

04 03 02 01 5 4 3 2

Library of Congress Cataloging-in-Publication Data

Barker, Judith

Stenciling & embossing greeting cards / by Judith Barker.

p. cm.

Includes index.

ISBN 0-89134-997-9 (pbk. : alk.)

1. Greeting cards. 2. Stencil work. 3. Rubber stamp printing. 4. Embossing (Printing)

I. Title: Stenciling and embossing greeting cards. II. Title.

TT872.B38 2000

745.594'1--dc21

00-020011

Editor: Jane Friedman

Interior Designer: Amber Traven

Production artist: Donna Cozatchy

Production coordinator: John L. Peavler

Photographers: Christine Polomsky and Al Parrish

CREDITS

The following people deserve credit for helping design the listed cards.

Gail Rundgren	Shrink Plastic Ornament Card, Paper Tole Tulip, Cut-and-Pierce Tulip Wreath Photo Card, Cutout Teapot Notecard, Sponged Vellum Tulip Card, Halloween Watercolor Card
Anita Bechman	Dried Floral Embossed Card
Barbara Swanson	Woodburned Teddy Postcard
Heidi James	Clay and Crinkle Sun Card
Colleen Pondelli	Hummingbird Music Card, Foil Ornament Card, Glossy Snowflake Card, Gold-Embellished Fleur-de-lis, Overlay Rose on Handmade Paper, Double-Embossed Glossy Leaves, Chinese Character Card, Angel Watercolor Card With Matching Envelope
Christine Angeli	Glittery Star Card

ACKNOWLEDGMENTS

The focused attention of a few of my co-workers enabled us to accomplish all the projects in this book. It was exciting to plan and experiment with various media; the unexpected results were found to be quite satisfying. Gail Rundgren and Colleen Pondelli were my four working hands and ceaselessly tapped, embossed, sprayed, cut, glued and stenciled.

It was relaxing to finally put it all together as Christine Polomsky photographed the projects, and Nicole Klungle and Jane Friedman methodically and meditatively assisted as the process unfolded. I truly had one of the most pleasant and relaxing periods in my life as I guided this book through its completion.

I hope you will discover new and exciting innovative uses for stencils and have a wonderful time enjoying the creative periods surrounding the creation of these beautiful handmade cards.

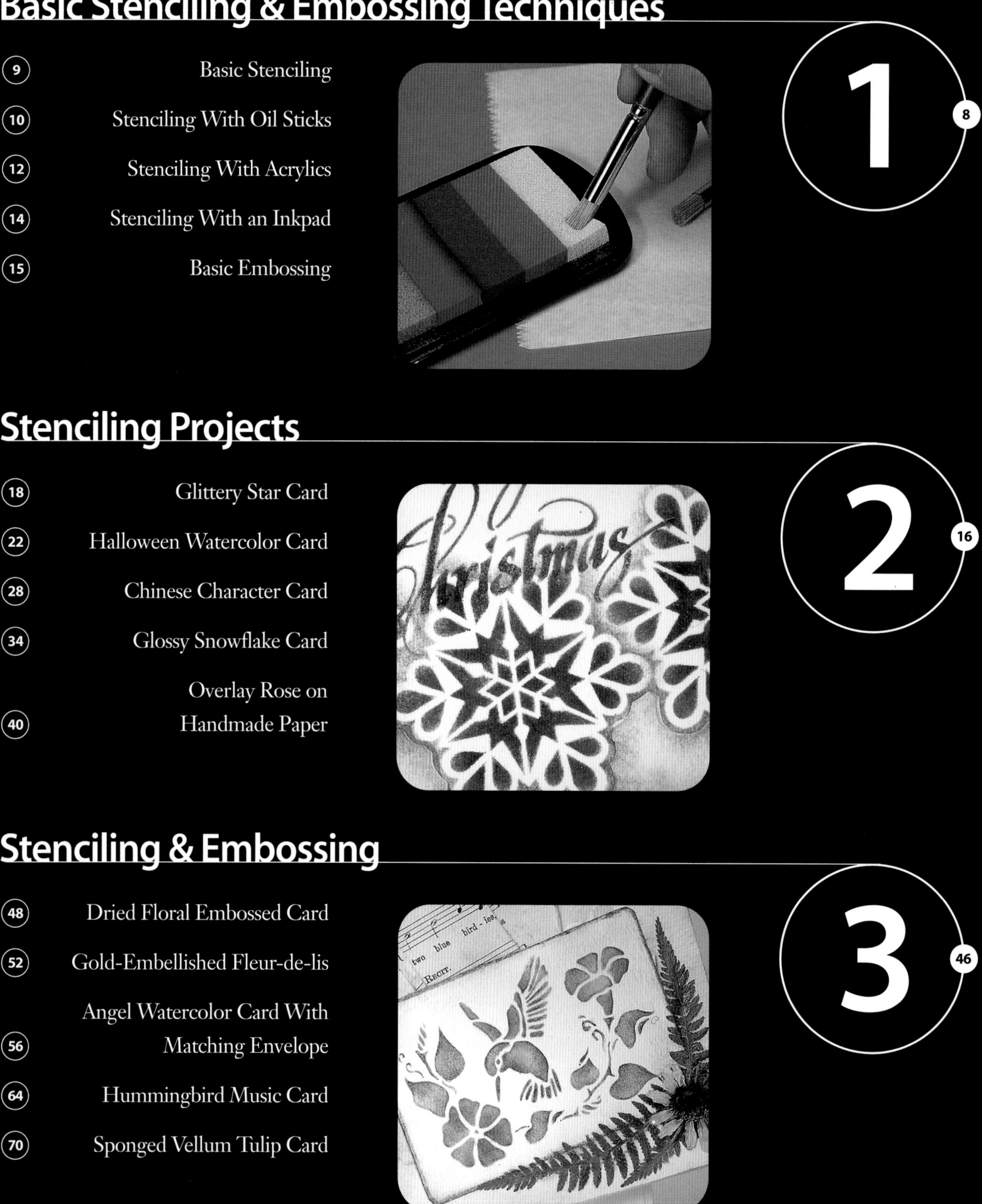

Basic Stenciling & Embossing Techniques

Stenciling Projects

Stenciling & Embossing

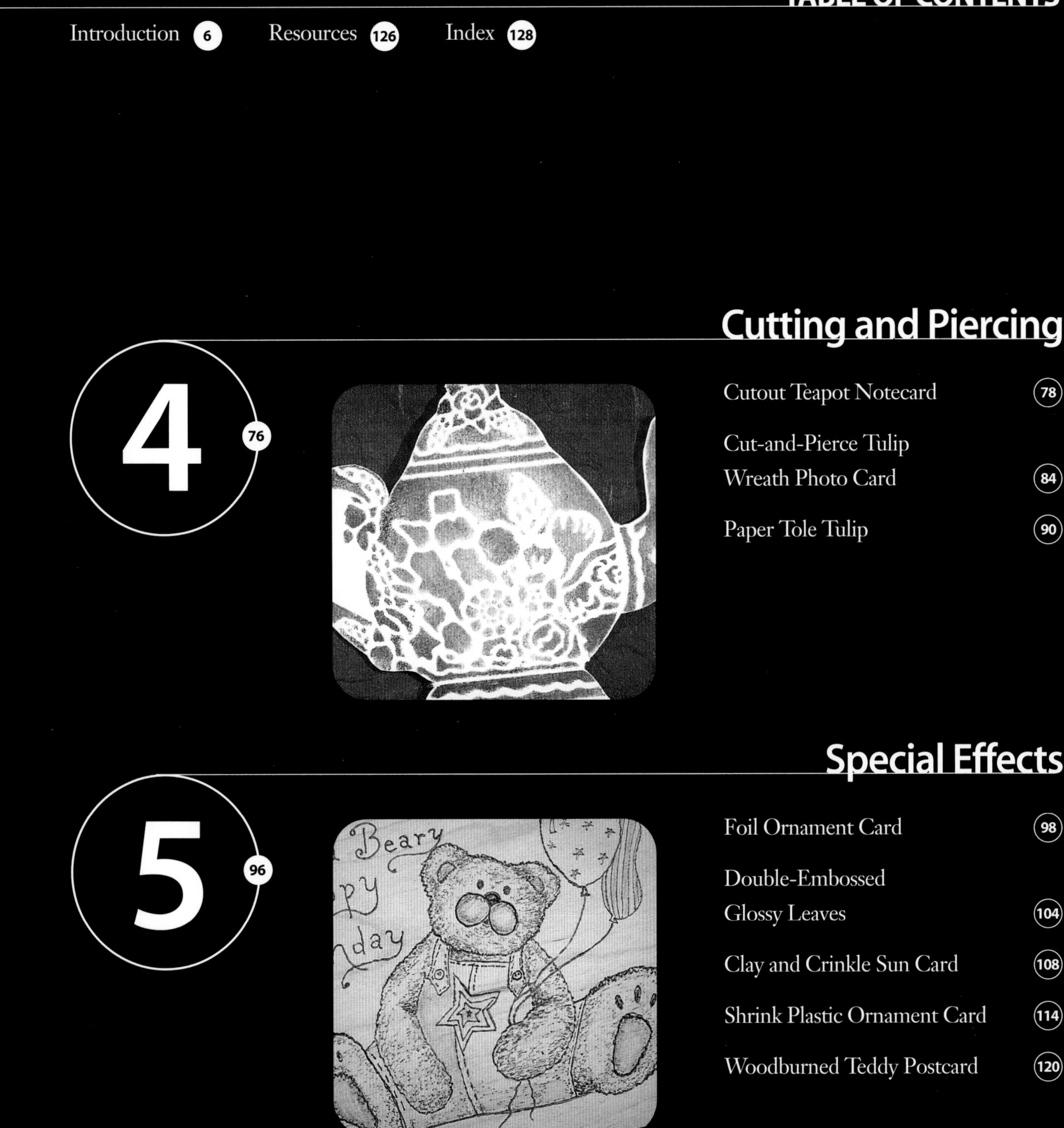

Cutting and Piercing

4 76

Special Effects

5 96

Two blue bird ·
two blue bird - ies,
RECIT.

Stenciling and embossing are so easy and relaxing. Stamp pad ink and oil sticks are foolproof! You can make a card in minutes. Everyone loves to receive handmade cards and the giver personally benefits from the satisfaction of creating a beautiful card.

A stencil can be cut quickly from any paper or plastic material with an art knife or manicure scissors. We've provided designs for your convenience. You may enlarge them on a copier and cut stencils from the photocopies. Stencils may be found in many stores, including rubber stamp stores, art and craft supply stores, and home decorating centers. Each type of material has its specific traits. American Traditional's blue laser stencils are extremely durable with fine detail. You can use them to stencil with any paint and on any surface. You can also use them for embossing.

There are so many ways to use stencils to decorate not only greeting cards but your whole world! Begin with a card for a friend and progressively pursue more extravagant projects. Soon your entire house could be a work of art!

Happy stenciling!

You will need the same basic materials for all stenciling projects. First, you'll need a stencil. For these examples, we used American Traditional stencil MS-84 Iris. There are many types of paint used in stenciling, including some paints made specifically for this purpose. Throughout this book, I have used oil sticks and bottled acrylic paints. You also need brushes with which to apply the color through the stencil. I use 3⁄16-inch stencil brushes, which should be available in your local art and craft supply store. You can use many different materials for your palette: a foam plate for acrylics, wax paper for oil sticks or even scrap paper. Keep paper towels on hand for rubbing extra color out of your stencil brush and use masking tape to secure your stencil to the stenciling surface. Be sure to tap the tape against your clothing a few times before adhering the stencil to paper; this decreases the adhesive strength of the tape and prevents it from tearing your paper.

a

Basic Stenciling and Embossing Techniques

BASIC STENCILING

Basic stenciling materials include stencil, cardstock or other stenciling surface, stencil brushes, palettes, acrylic paints, oil sticks and ink pads.

Stencils

MS-84. To make a stencil, photocopy this image at 80 percent and use a sharp craft knife to cut out the design. a

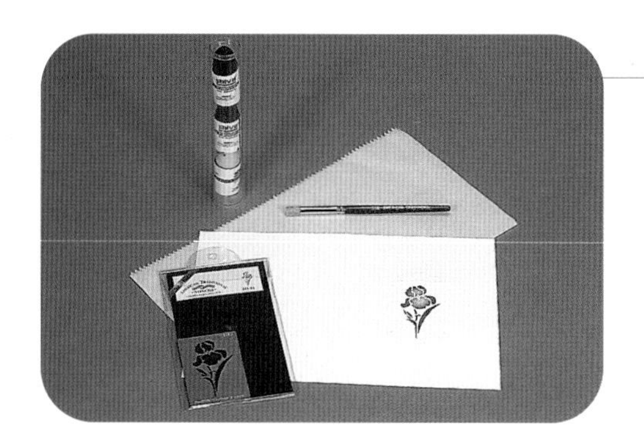

Stenciling With Oil Sticks

This exercise uses Shiva Paintstiks in Azo Yellow, Naphthol Red and Ultramarine Blue. These three colors come together in Shiva's primary colors kit. Use wax paper for a palette when stenciling with oil sticks.

1 Prepare palette

Remove the skin from the tip of an oil stick with a paper towel. Rub the stick on a wax paper palette to create a smear of color.

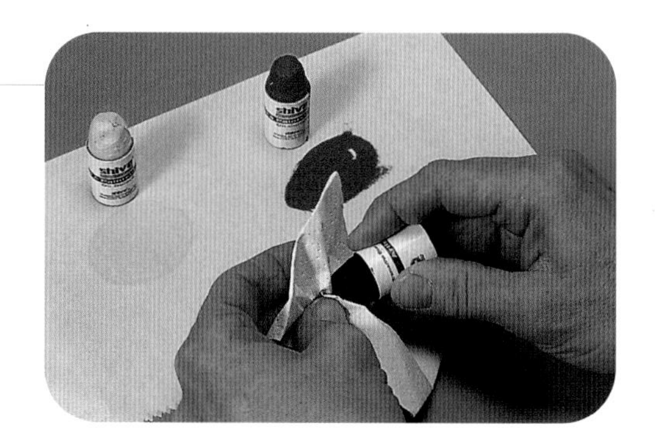

Load brush 2

Rub brush into the lightest color—in this case, Azo Yellow.

3 Start stenciling

Tap brush through stencil. You can also rub gently in a circular motion.

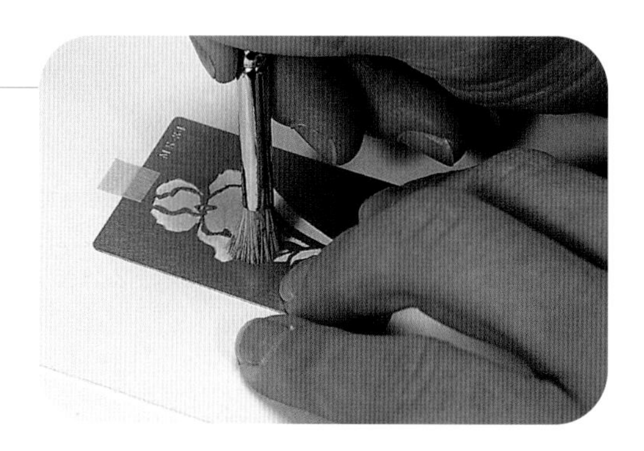

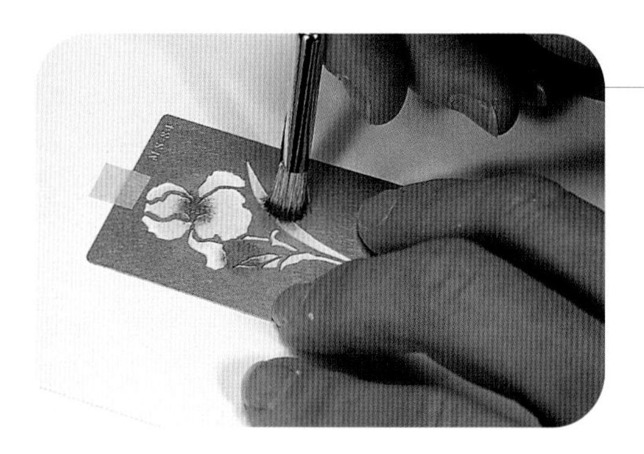

Add red 4

Tap or rub in accents in red.

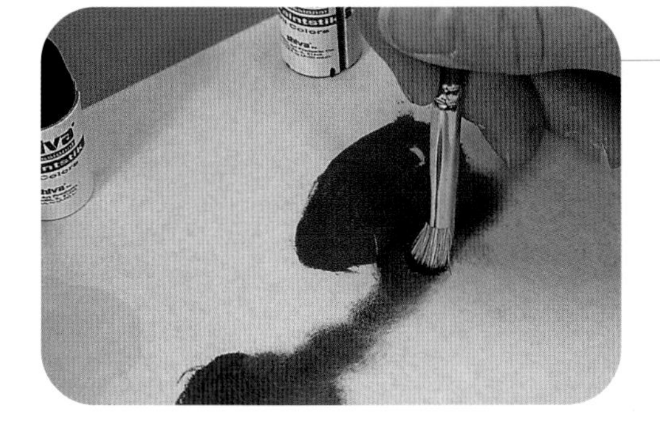

Mix purple

Mix colors by blending on palette. Red and blue make purple.

6 Add purple

Tap or rub in purple.

Mix green

Yellow and blue make green.

8 Add green

Stencil green last because it can turn other colors muddy. A little green in the center of the iris will add depth.

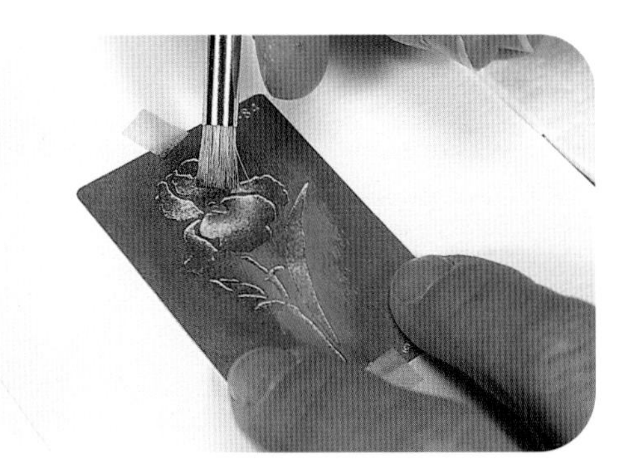

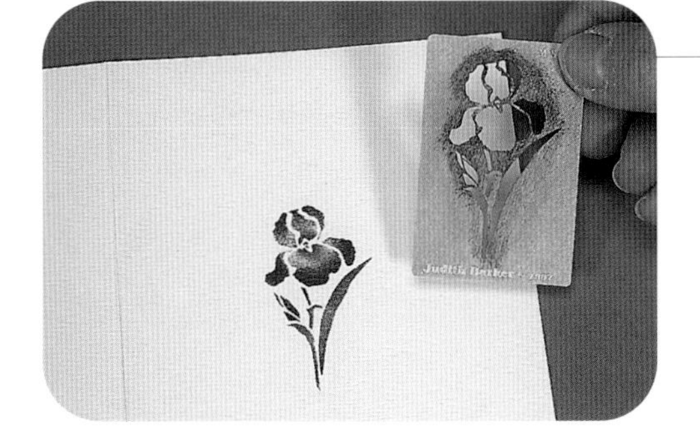

Finished iris

Remove your stencil, then clean it with a dry cloth or paper towel.

Stenciling With Acrylics

You'll need a small container of water and a foam palette when using acrylics. For this exercise, we used DecoArt Americana acrylics in Yellow Light, Brandy Wine, Wedgewood Blue and Avocado.

1 Moisten brush

Dip brush in water to moisten bristles.

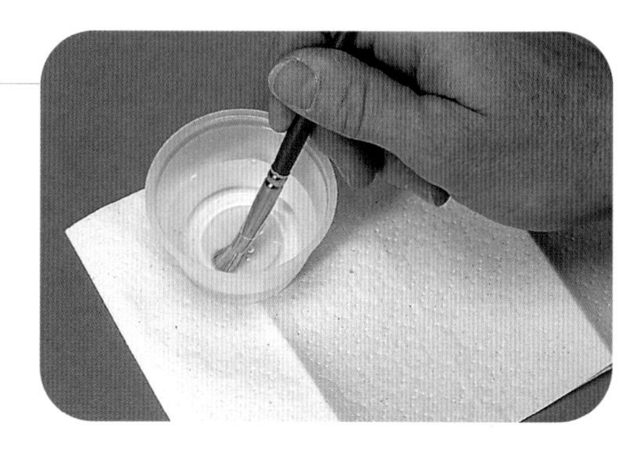

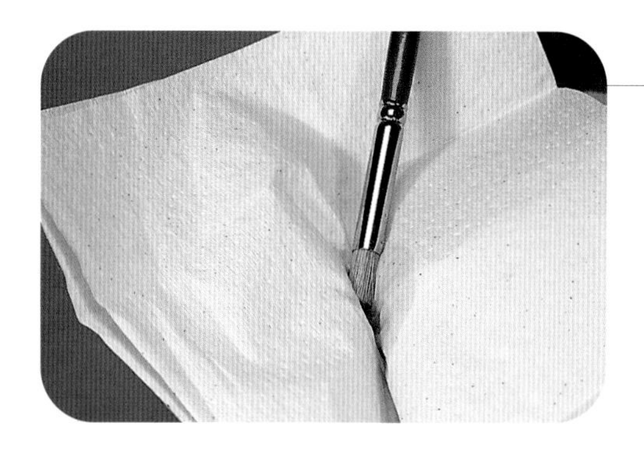

Dry the brush 2

Squeeze out excess water on a paper towel.

3 Pick up paint and rub out

Squeeze a small dollop of each color onto a foam plate (or other suitable palette). Dip brush into the lightest color first, Yellow Light. Rub out on paper towel to remove all but a trace of paint from the brush.

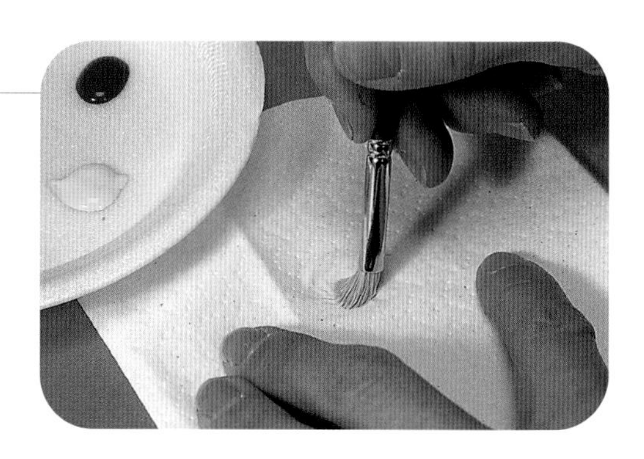

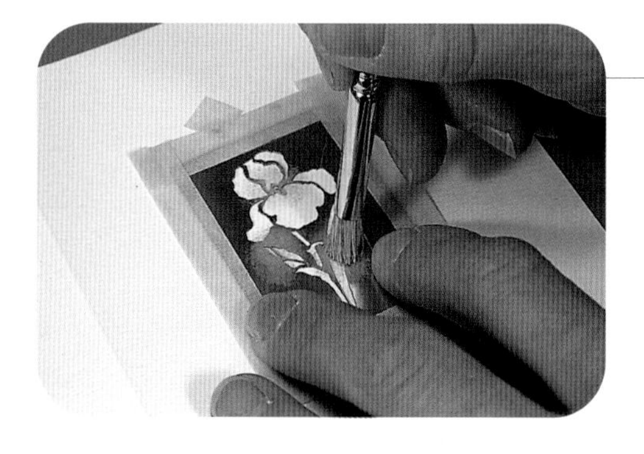

Begin stenciling 4

Tap or rub yellow into the stencil. Rinse brush between colors and dry with paper towel.

Mix purple 5

To make purple, first tap into red paint and rub out.

6 Mix purple

Then tap into blue and rub out, mixing colors on the brush.

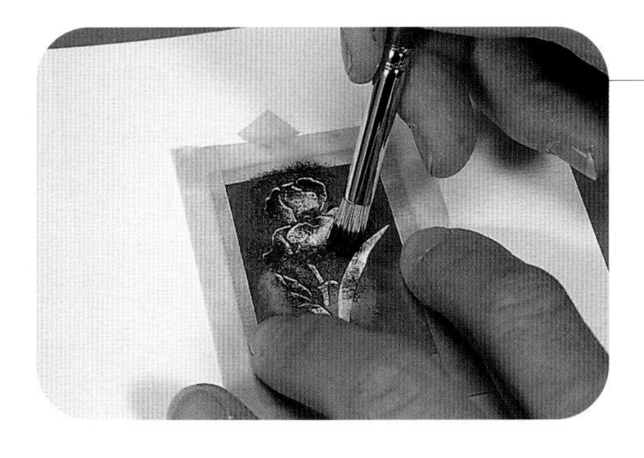

Add purple 7

Tap or rub purple into stencil.

8 Add green

As usual, finish with green.

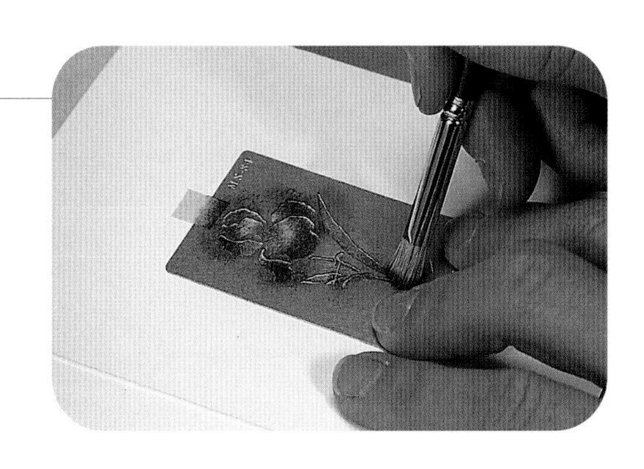

Finished iris

Remove the stencil, then clean with hot water and a nylon scouring pad.

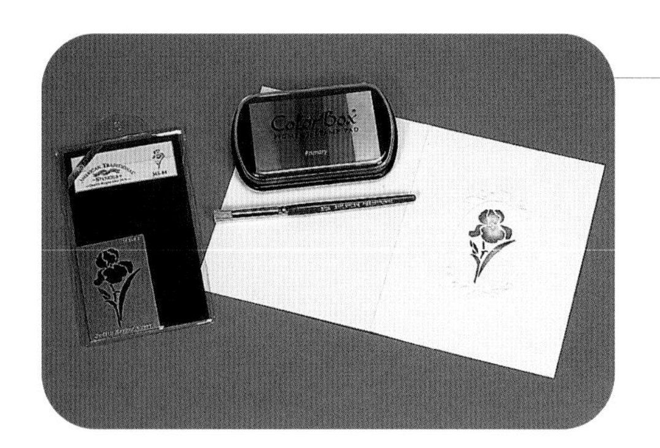

Stenciling With an Inkpad

A multicolored ink pad is a convenient stenciling tool. Here I'm using Color Box's Primary pigment stamp pad. Use a separate brush for each color, except when mixing.

1 Load brush

Tap brush into pad. Start with the lightest color.

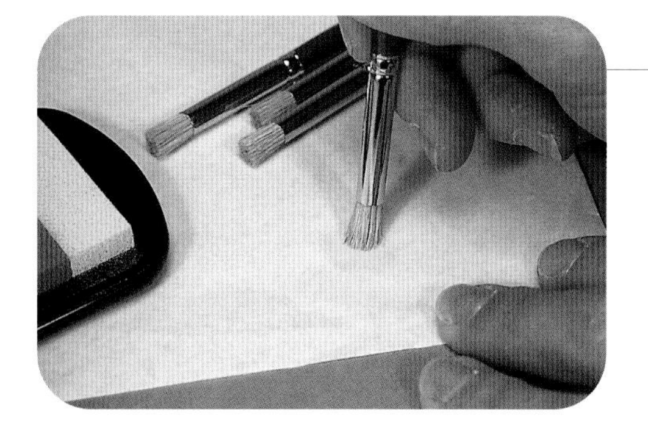

Rub out 2

Tap off or rub out excess color on scrap paper or paper towel.

3 Add color

Tap or rub color through stencil.

Mix color 4

To mix colors, tap into one color and then the other. Mix on the brush by rubbing in a circular motion on scrap paper or paper towel.

Iris stenciled in four different color combinations.

BASIC EMBOSSING

I used American Traditional stencil BL-35 Rose for this exercise. It's easiest to emboss using a light box because you can see the outline of the stencil under your paper. You can also emboss by feel without a light box. A stylus or embossing tool has a ball tip at one end for outlining. You'll also need masking tape to adhere the stencil to your cardstock.

a

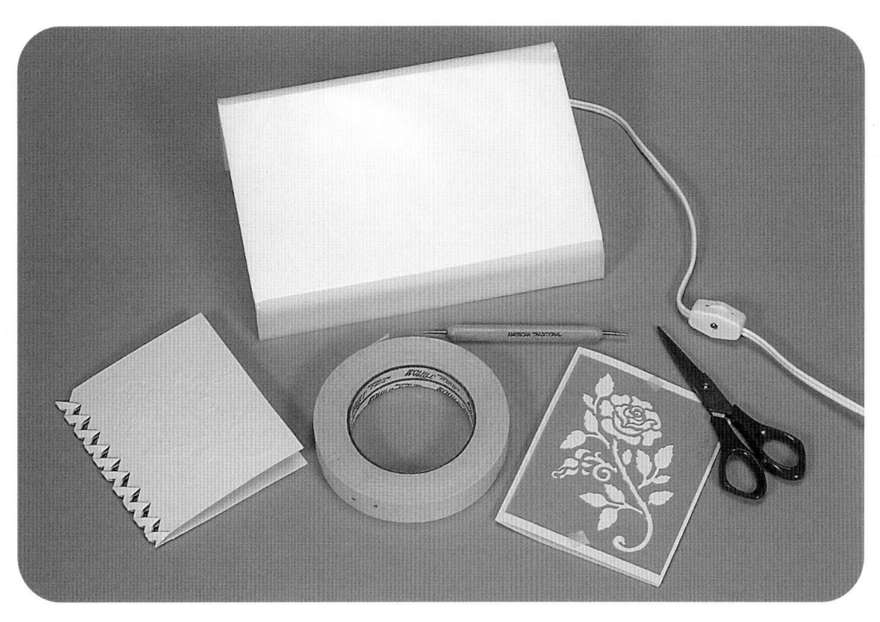

Emboss

Attach the stencil to the front of the card with two ¼-inch pieces of masking tape. Flip the card over onto the light box (or use a lamp under a glass table or a piece of clear plastic ware). Rub your fingers over the paper before embossing; the oil from your hand will help the stylus glide more easily. From the back of the paper, trace the entire outline of the stencil with the stylus.

Stencils

BL-35. To make a stencil, photocopy this image at 167 percent and use a sharp craft knife to cut out the design. (a)

Merry Christmas
HAPPY HALLOWEEN
BOO!
LOVE

Stenciling Projects

Now that you understand the basic principles of stenciling, it's time to get creative. These cards feature many types of stencils and several different stenciling mediums. You'll learn a few techniques to jazz up your designs—stenciling is more than just paint on paper! I have provided stencil patterns for every project in this book. Photocopy them to the proper size, then cut out with a sharp craft knife or scissors. Cuticle scissors work well. Once you have the design cut out of paper, you can use it as is or transfer it to heavier plastic, acetate or Mylar. See the resources guide at the end of the book for information on where you can purchase stencils and stenciling supplies. Stencil away!

Glittery Star Card

This glittery card sure looks impressive, but it couldn't be easier. Instead of stenciling with paint, stencil the stars with glue and then top with glitter. Don't be afraid to try this project with different colors and types of paper and with all sorts of different stencils.

Materials

- American Traditional stencil
  - BL-445 Hearts, Stars, and Dots
- Paper
  - 5½" x 4¼" white notecard
  - 5½" x 4¼" shiny black paper
  - 5½" x 4¼" shiny gold paper
- tacky glue
- copper, emerald and purple glitter
- 3/16" stencil brush
- Fiskars decorative edging scissors
- glue stick
- eraser pencil (for correcting errors and cleaning up edges)

BL-445. To make a stencil, photocopy this image at 111 percent and use a sharp craft knife to cut out the design. 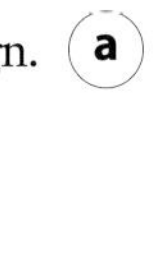

1 Prepare cardstock and paper

Glue the shiny gold paper to the front of your white cardstock to cover entire front of card. Trim the edges of the shiny black paper with the decorative edging scissors so it is about ¼-inch smaller on each side than the size of the cardstock.

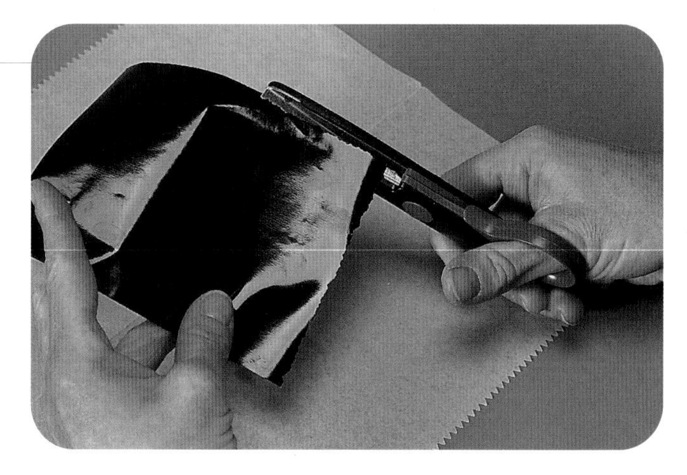

2 Add glue to palette

Squeeze out small amount of glue onto wax paper.

3 Stencil star

Stencil a star in the size of your choice on the black paper with glue.

4 Add first glitter color

Sprinkle glitter liberally over the wet glue while stencil is still on top of the paper.

5 Make multicolored star

Make a multicolored star by sprinkling half with one color of glitter and half with another color (shake off excess between colors). You can repeat this process several times with different sizes of stars. Stencil and glitter one star at a time.

Glue star to notecard 6

Carefully remove stencil. Allow to dry thoroughly. Attach the black paper with star to the front of the notecard with glue stick.

The finished card

Halloween Watercolor Card

This card is simple enough that older children can make it. Zig 2-Way glue has a no-mess applicator that makes it easy to get creative with glitter accents.

Materials

- American Traditional stencil:
  BL-172 Halloween Memories
- Paper
  5½" x 4¼" white notecard with matching envelope
- watercolor paints in basic colors
- foam makeup applicator sponge
- 3/16" stencil brush
- small container of water
- Zig 2-Way glue
- light-colored glitter
- masking tape

BL-172. To make a stencil, photocopy this image at 80 percent and use a sharp craft knife to cut out the design. (a)

1 Affix stencil to notecard

Center stencil on front of notecard. Tap a piece of masking tape on your clothing several times to make it less sticky, then tape the stencil in place.

2 Prepare sponge

Wet sponge and squeeze out excess water.

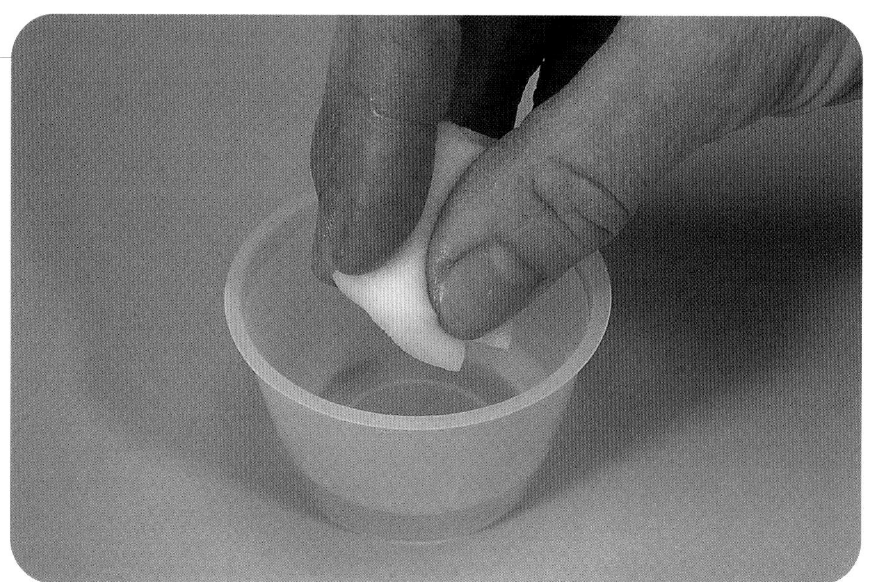

3 Load sponge

Dip sponge into yellow watercolor.

Test paint consistency 4

Test paint consistency on scrap paper. You don't want the paint so heavy or runny that it will bleed under the stencil. Add more paint or water as needed, keeping in mind that only a very small amount of paint should remain on the sponge.

Add color with sponge 5

Tap the nearly dry sponge along the edge of the stencil to make a colored border.

Load brush with black 6

Dip the stencil brush in water, tap dry on a piece of scrap paper, and dip it into black watercolor. Test the consistency on scrap paper and add paint or water as needed.

7 Stencil black

Stencil as desired in black, and add a little black around the stencil border.

8 Remove stencil

9 Load brush with orange

Rinse brush in water and add orange, blotting out on paper towel. Drybrush orange over witch's face, pumpkin, witch's brew and words.

Add glue accents (10)

Apply glue to select areas, such as eyes, cauldron bubbles and words.

Add glitter (11)

Sprinkle glitter over the glue and shake off excess.

The finished card

Chinese Character Card

Chinese characters are as beautiful as they are meaningful. This card features the character for love. The colors, simplicity, and class of this card make it perfect for a man or woman.

Materials

- American Traditional stencil:
  BL-167 Love
- Paper
  10¾" x 6" black cardstock
  folded to 5⅜" x 6"
  5½" x 4¼" red cardstock
  5½" x 4¼" white linen paper
  5½" x 6" white mulberry paper
- Shiva Paintstik in Black
- tacky glue
- gold embossing powder
- $^{3}/_{16}$" stencil brushes
- heat gun
- wax paper
- masking tape

BL-167. To make a stencil, photocopy this image at 61 percent and use a sharp craft knife to cut out the design. (a)

1 Stencil black

Center your stencil on red cardstock with masking tape. Stencil using black oil stick. Remove the stencil and clean it with a paper towel. Allow stenciling to dry.

Reposition stencil 2

Reapply stencil over lettering, but offset by about ⅛ inch down and to the right.

3 Stencil with glue

Squeeze a small amount of glue onto wax paper or scrap paper. Brush the edges of the character and lettering with glue. Remove stencil.

Add gold powder 4

Apply gold embossing powder. Shake off the excess and return it to the jar.

5 Heat

Heat the embossing powder with the heat gun until it melts.

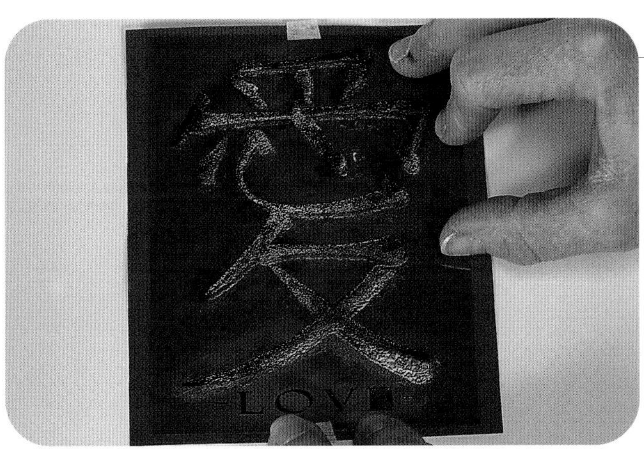

Reposition stencil 6

Tape stencil to the cardstock in its original position.

7 Blend in black

Stencil in black along the top edges of the lettering, blending from black to gold.

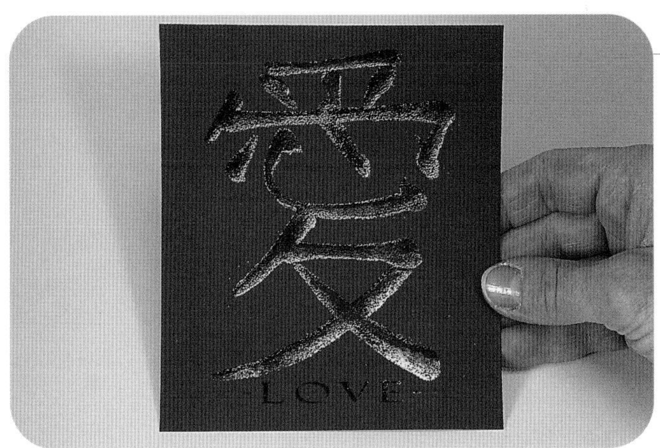

Remove stencil 8

Lettering should appear three-dimensional with gold highlights.

9 Add stenciling to black cardstock

Fold black cardstock in half to measure 6" x 5⅜". Center and glue the stenciled red card onto the black cardstock.

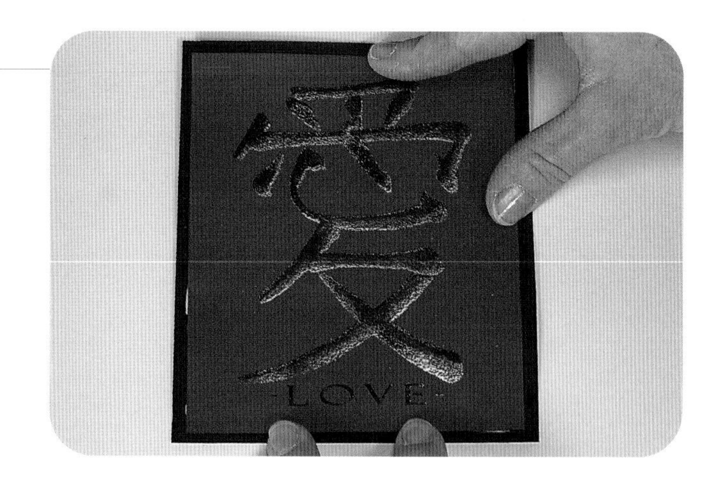

Line notecard 10

Open card. Apply a thin line of glue down the center of the left flap and attach a sheet of mulberry paper.

11 Deckle the linen paper

Carefully tear the edges of the linen paper to get a deckled edge.

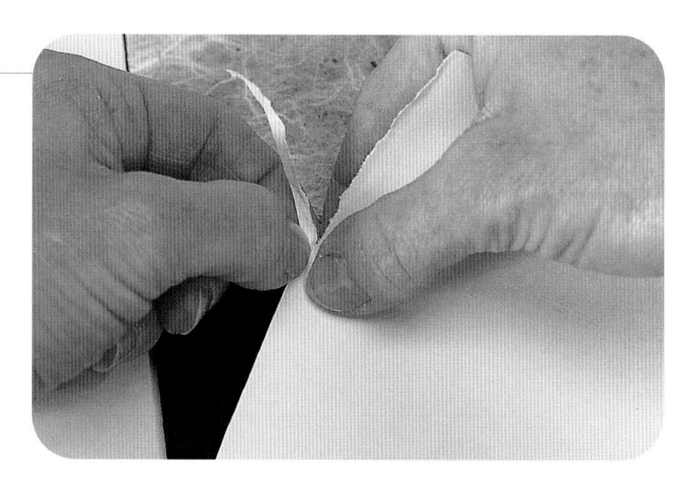

Drybrush with black 12

Drybrush the deckled edges with the stencil brush and the black oil stick.

13 Line the right side of the card

Glue the linen paper into the inside of the card to create a writing surface.

The finished card

Glossy Snowflake Card

Use clear embossing powder on this card to add a subtle glint to the design. The embossing powder creates a glossy surface that contrasts with the matte paper surrounding the snowflakes.

Materials

- American Traditional stencils
  - FS-957 Snowflake Ornament
  - GS-139 Merry Christmas
- Paper
  - 5½" x 4¼" white note card with matching envelope
- Shiva Paintstiks
  - Azo Yellow
  - Naphthol Red
  - Prussian Blue
  - Sap Green
- four 3/16" stencil brushes
- clear embossing powder
- heat gun
- scissors
- Fiskars scallop decorative edging scissors
- wax paper
- masking tape

F-957. To make a stencil, photocopy this image at 70 percent and use a sharp craft knife to cut out the design. **a**

GS-139. To make a stencil, photocopy this image at 70 percent and use a sharp craft knife to cut out the design. **b**

a

Merry Christmas

b

1 Stencil first snowflake

Stencil snowflake in Prussian Blue on bottom center of card front.

2 Add more snowflakes

Repeat process on both sides of center snowflake, positioning the additional snowflakes slightly higher.

3 Add embossing powder

Sprinkle embossing powder over snowflakes. Shake off excess powder and return it to container.

Heat 

Melt embossing powder with heat gun.

Stencil message 5

Position "Merry Christmas" stencil (or a stencil with a message of your choice) on the center of the card front, overlapping snowflakes slightly. Tape into place and stencil with a mixture of Azo Yellow, Naphthol Red and Sap Green.

Add embossing powder and heat 6

Sprinkle embossing powder over the lettering, returning excess to jar. Melt the powder with a heat gun.

7 Trim

Trim around snowflakes along bottom edge of card.

8 Create snowflake mask

To create a wax paper mask from the snowflake stencil, begin by stenciling a snowflake lightly onto wax paper. Carefully cut out the snowflake.

9 Drybrush blue

Place wax paper snowflake over snowflakes on card and drybrush with Prussian Blue around the edges of the snowflakes. The mask keeps paint from getting on the snowflakes themselves.

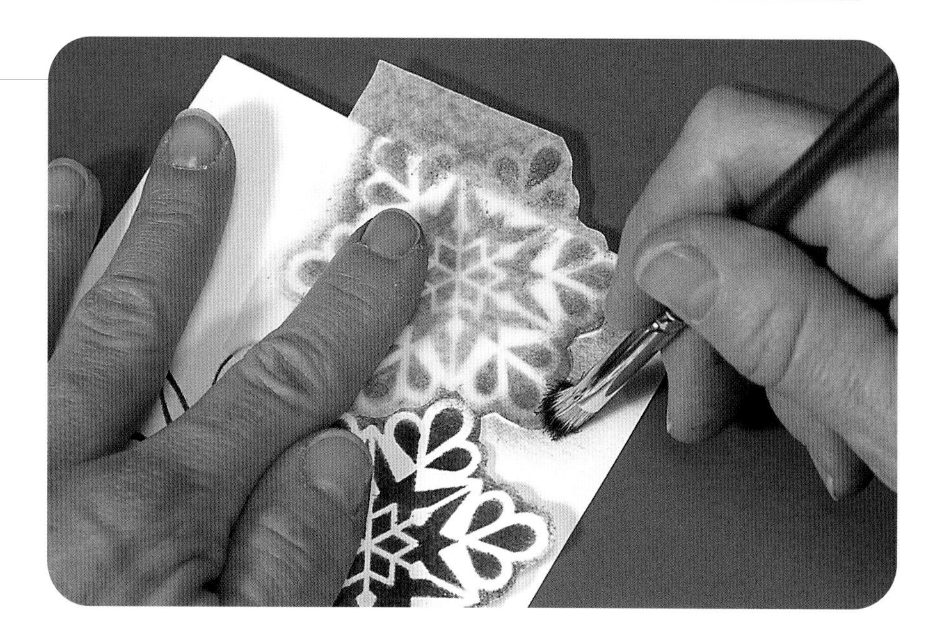

Decorate envelope

Decorate envelope flap to match the card. Use scallop edging scissors to trim the edge of the flap.

Overlay Rose on Handmade Paper

The stencil for this project comes in three parts, each of which is stenciled separately. On the purchased stencils, you will notice a triangular hole in each corner. These registration marks allow you to position each stencil exactly in line with the others. Place small pieces of masking tape on your stenciling surface underneath the registration marks, then trace inside the registration marks. Align the registration marks for the next stencil overlay with your first marks, and voilà! You're ready to stencil.

Materials

- American Traditional stencil
  - CS-7 Three-Part Rose
- Paper
  - 5" x 6" white mulberry handmade paper
  - 6" x 7" dark teal textured paper
- Shiva Paintstiks
  - Azo Yellow
  - Naphthol Red
  - Prussian Blue
  - Sap Green
- four $\frac{3}{16}$" stencil brushes
- masking tape
- wax paper

CS-7. Part 1. To make a stencil, photocopy this image at 133 percent and use a sharp craft knife to cut out the design. (a)

CS-7. Part 2. To make a stencil, photocopy this image at 133 percent and use a sharp craft knife to cut out the design. (b)

CS-7. Part 3. To make a stencil, photocopy this image at 133 percent and use a sharp craft knife to cut out the design. (c)

1 Fringe handmade paper

To "fringe" the edges of the handmade paper, start by dipping a brush or rolled-up paper towel in water. Wet a ¼-inch border around the handmade paper.

Pull fringe 2

Allow the water to soak in for several seconds, then pull edges gently with fingernails.

3 Position stencil

Attach part 1 of the rose stencil to the handmade paper with masking tape. If you are using a purchased stencil, you will see a triangular registration opening in the corners of each part of the stencil. Place small pieces of tape on the handmade paper under the registration openings.

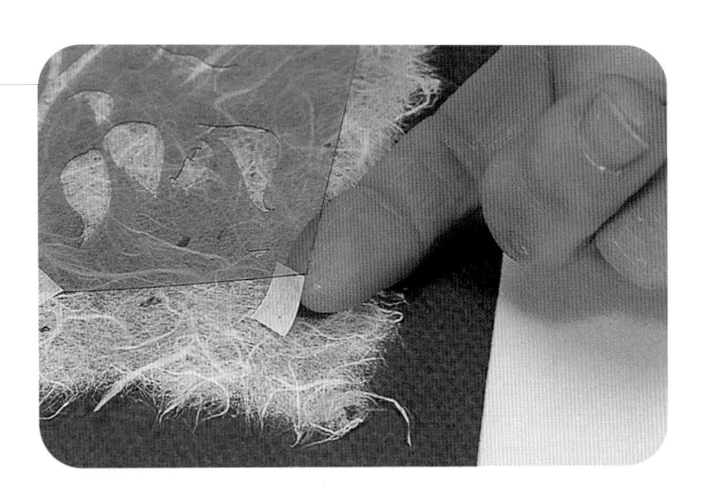

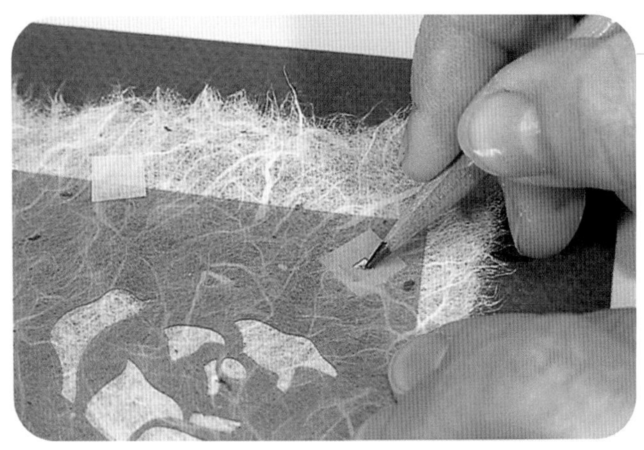

Mark registration 4

Mark the masking tape with pencil through the registration openings.

5 Begin stenciling

Use the image on page 45 as a color guide and begin stenciling the image. Your first color should be the lightest, Azo Yellow.

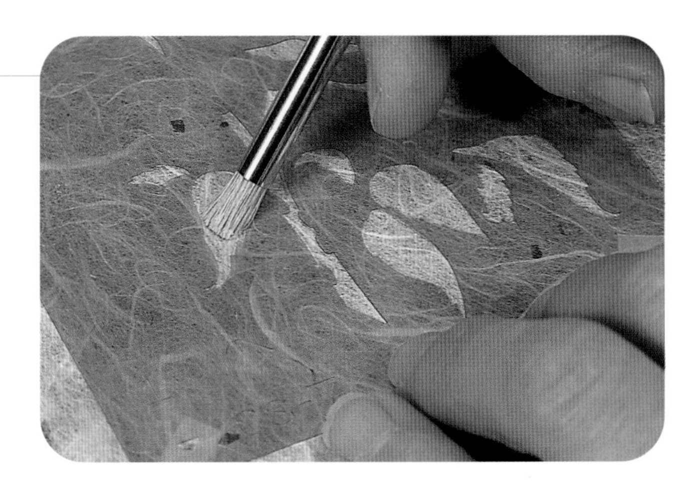

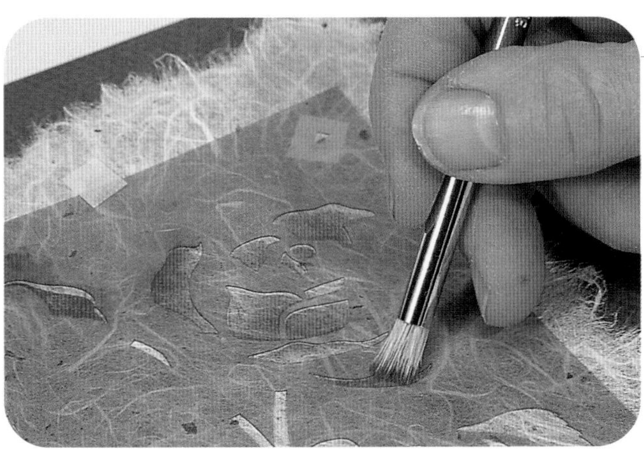

Add red and green 6

Continue stenciling with red, then move on to green. Remember that green should always be stenciled last. To make different shades of green, use green alone or over yellow or blue. You can also blend your own green on the palette from Prussian Blue and Azo Yellow.

7 Remove part 1

Remove part 1 of the rose stencil, leaving masking tape with registration marks in place.

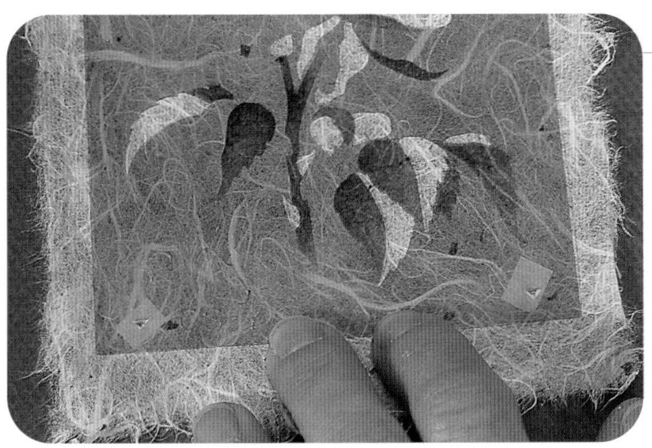

Stencil part 2 8

Position part 2 of the rose stencil so that the registration openings fall directly over the registration marks on the masking tape. Tape in place. Stencil with yellow, then red and green.

9 Remove part 2

Remove the second part of the stencil, again leaving the masking tape registration marks on the paper.

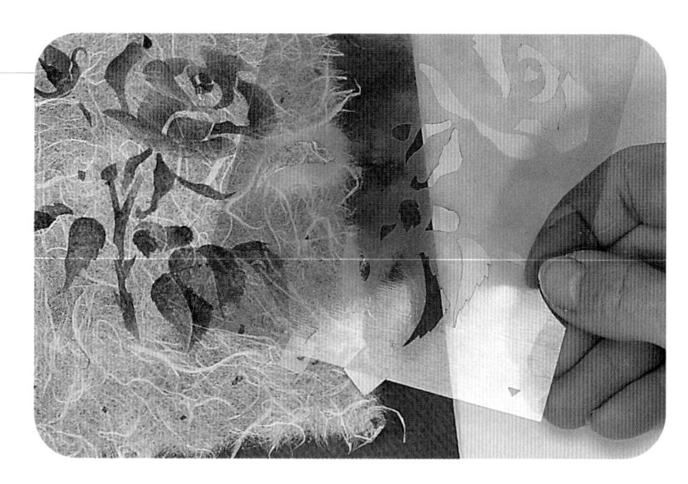

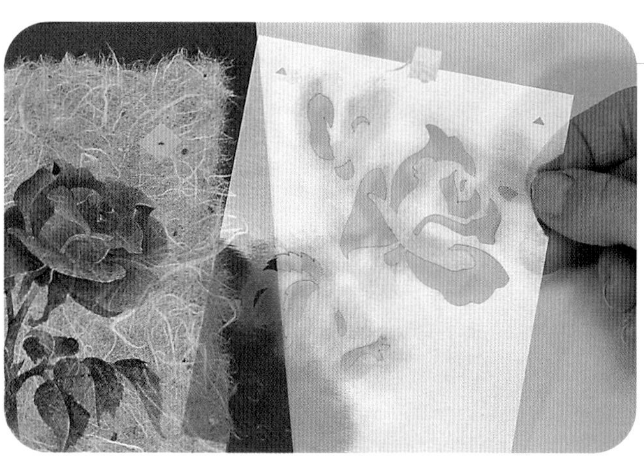

Stencil part 3 10

Position part 3 of the stencil and align the registration marks. Stencil with yellow, red, then green. Remove the stencil when done.

11 Remove registration marks

Carefully remove the masking tape registration marks from the handmade paper. Glue the stenciled paper to teal background paper.

The finished card

Color guide for rose

The earth laughs with flowers.
Ralph Waldo Emerson

3

Stenciling and Embossing Projects

It's time to add another element to our stenciled greeting card projects. Embossing creates a raised image that may or may not be stenciled as well. An embossing tool, with its rounded tip, is essential for good results; it embosses the paper without tearing it. You should be able to find this tool in art and craft supply stores and rubber stamp stores. Some paper stores may also carry this tool. Most stencils can be used for embossing, as long as they are cut from a thicker, relatively stiff material. If you are cutting your own stencils for embossing, be sure to choose a heavy plastic or acetate for your stencil material rather than paper. A woodburning tool or other hot-tipped cutting tool is useful for cutting stencils from plastic. Most of these projects call for a light box. Since the stencil is placed under the paper for embossing, working over a light box makes it easier to see the pattern you will be embossing. If you do not have a light box, place a small lamp under a glass table. You can also emboss without a light box, being careful to feel the outline of the stencil as you are following it. This is necessary when using dark, opaque papers.

Dried Floral Embossed Card

The dried flowers add an elegant touch to this embossed card—or is it the embossing that adds an elegant touch to this floral card? You'll be pleased with the way both elements work together to create a colorful and soft impression.

Materials

- American Traditional stencil
  MS-213 Blossoms & Ivy
- Paper
  5½" x 4¼" white notecard
- embossing tool
- light box
- clear-drying glue
- clear contact paper
- scissors
- dried small pressed flowers and greens
- pen or rubber stamp (optional, for lettering)
- masking tape

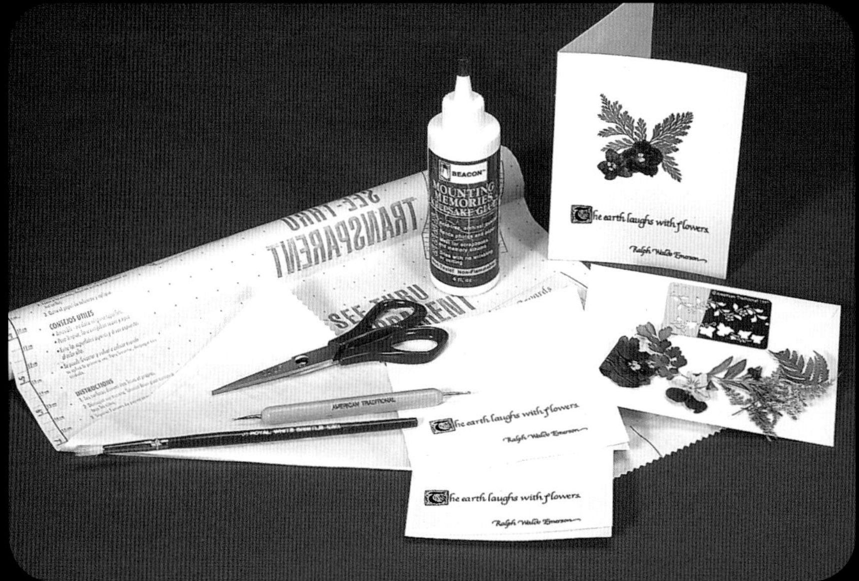

MS-213. To make a stencil, photocopy this image at 50 percent and use a sharp craft knife to cut out the design. (a)

1 Write message and position stencil

Hand-write or stamp your message at the bottom of the card front. Tape the stencil at the top of the card as shown. We will use only the blossom portion of the stencil for this project.

Emboss cardstock 2

Once stencil is taped in place, flip the cardstock and stencil over and place on light source. Rub your fingers over the area to be embossed; the oil from your hands will make the embossing tool glide more easily. With your embossing tool, trace inside all the stencil openings.

3 Form border

Reposition stencil and emboss three more times, creating a frame for the dried flowers.

Add flowers 4

Glue the dried flowers in a pleasing arrangement inside the embossed frame. Use a brush to apply the glue.

5 **Finish flower arrangement**

Glue the greens down first, then add the flowers. Continue adding flowers until you get an attractive bouquet.

Seal with contact paper 6

Cut clear contact paper to the size of the card and adhere it to seal and preserve the dried flowers.

The finished card

Gold-Embellished Fleur-de-lis

The fleur-de-lis on this card is stenciled in yellow, covered with gold embossing powder, then bordered with embossed lines and diamonds. Embossing powder creates a raised glossy surface in imitation of the old-fashioned engraving of wedding invitations and calling cards. The matte finish of the black cardstock balances the fleur-de-lis design.

Materials

- American Traditional stencil
  - BL-155 Fleur d'lis
- Paper
  - 5½" x 4¼" black notecard
  - 4" x 5" red cardstock
  - 5½" x 4¼" white paper (optional, for inside of card)
- Shiva Paintstik in Azo Yellow
- 3/16" stencil brush
- gold embossing powder
- heat gun
- embossing tool
- scissors
- glue stick
- wax paper
- masking tape

BL-155. To make a stencil, photocopy this image at 59 percent and use a sharp craft knife to cut out the design. 

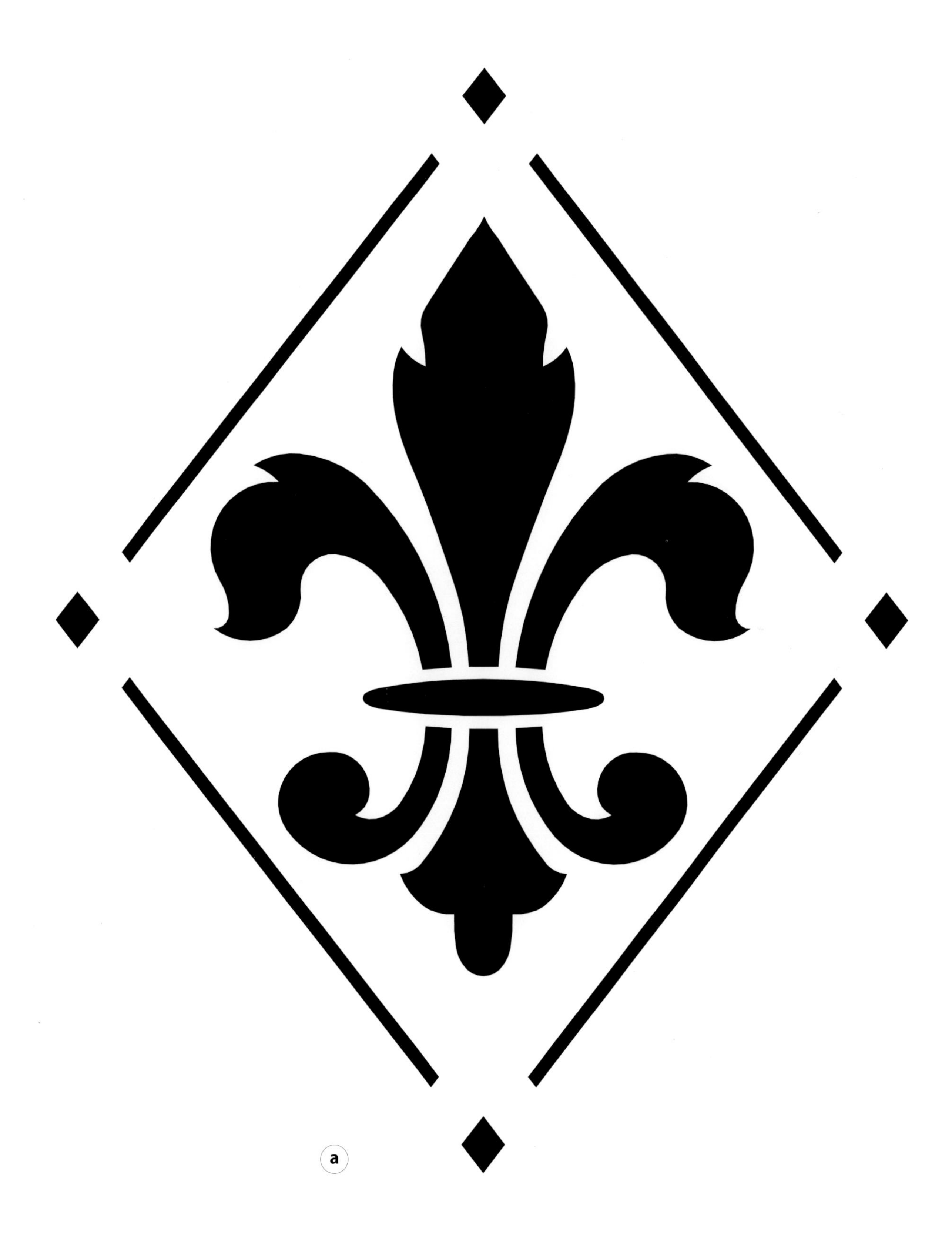

1 Stencil the fleur-de-lis

Rub the yellow oil stick onto your wax paper palette. Center the stencil and tape in place on the red cardstock. Tape off the lines and diamonds in the design to prevent paint from getting in these areas. Stencil the fleur-de-lis in yellow. Remove stencil.

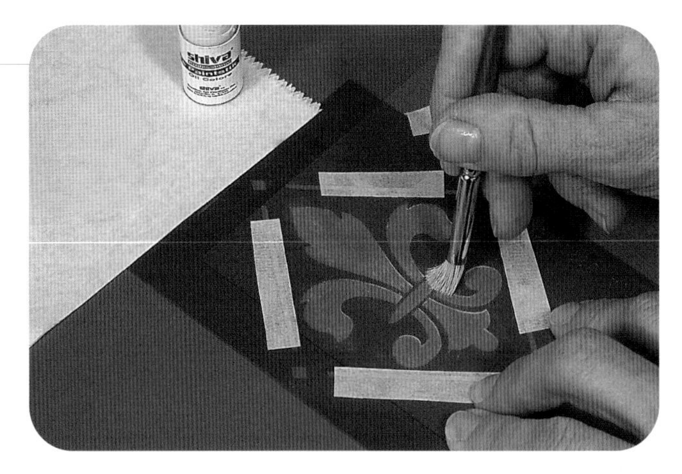

Add embossing powder 2

Pour gold embossing powder over the stenciled fleur-de-lis while the paint is still tacky. Remove excess powder and return to jar.

3 Heat

Heat the embossing powder, holding the heat gun about an inch above the design. The powder will melt and shine.

Cut out fleur-de-lis 4

Cut out the fleur-de-lis, leaving a narrow border of red paper.

5 Emboss the black notecard

Remove the tape from the lines and diamonds of the fleur-de-lis stencil. Center and attach the stencil to the front of the black notecard. Trace over the lines and diamonds. (Light won't show through the black paper, so you don't need a light box here.) Flip card over and emboss using your trace lines as a guide. Remove stencil.

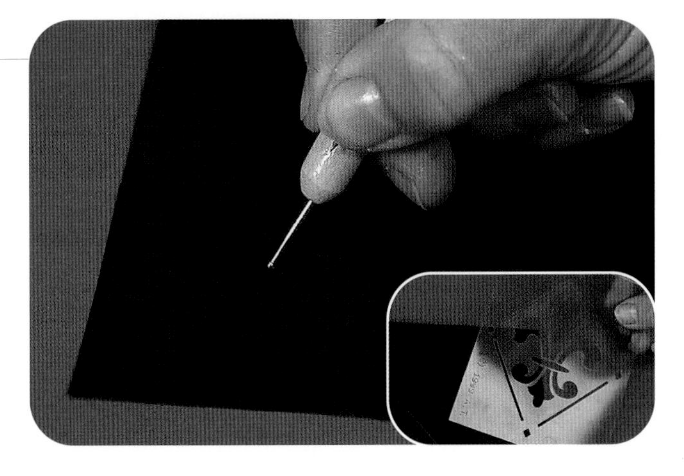

Apply glue stick 6

Apply glue stick to the edges on the back of the gold-and-red fleur-de-lis.

7 Attach fleur-de-lis to card

Center the fleur-de-lis inside the line-and-diamond embossed border and affix to the black cardstock.

Finish card 

To create a nice place to write your message, apply glue stick to the edges of the back of the white paper. Open the card and affix the paper to the right side.

Angel Watercolor Card With Matching Envelope

Creating this colorful card with watercolor paints is easier than it looks. There's no need to buy tubes of artist-grade watercolor—a child's watercolor set will work fine. For the envelope, you can decorate the plain white envelope that probably came with your notecard, or make your own using vellum and the envelope template and paint it to match your angel. The vellum envelope will remain transparent and is a unique touch.

Materials

- American Traditional stencils
  - BL-89 Angel
  - BL-442 Envelope Template
- Paper
  - 5½" x 4¼" white notecard and envelope
  - 5½" x 4¼" white vellum
  - 5½" x 4¼" lavender tissue paper
  - 8" x 10" white vellum (for envelope)
- watercolor paints in basic colors
- makeup applicator sponge
- small container of water
- small watercolor brush
- large watercolor brush
- embossing tool
- light box
- glue stick
- hole punch
- scissors
- 12" length of ½"-wide lavender ribbon
- masking tape

BL-89. To make a stencil, photocopy this image at 125 percent and use a sharp craft knife to cut out the design. (a)

BL-442. To make a stencil, photocopy this image at 167 percent and use a sharp craft knife to cut out the design. (b)

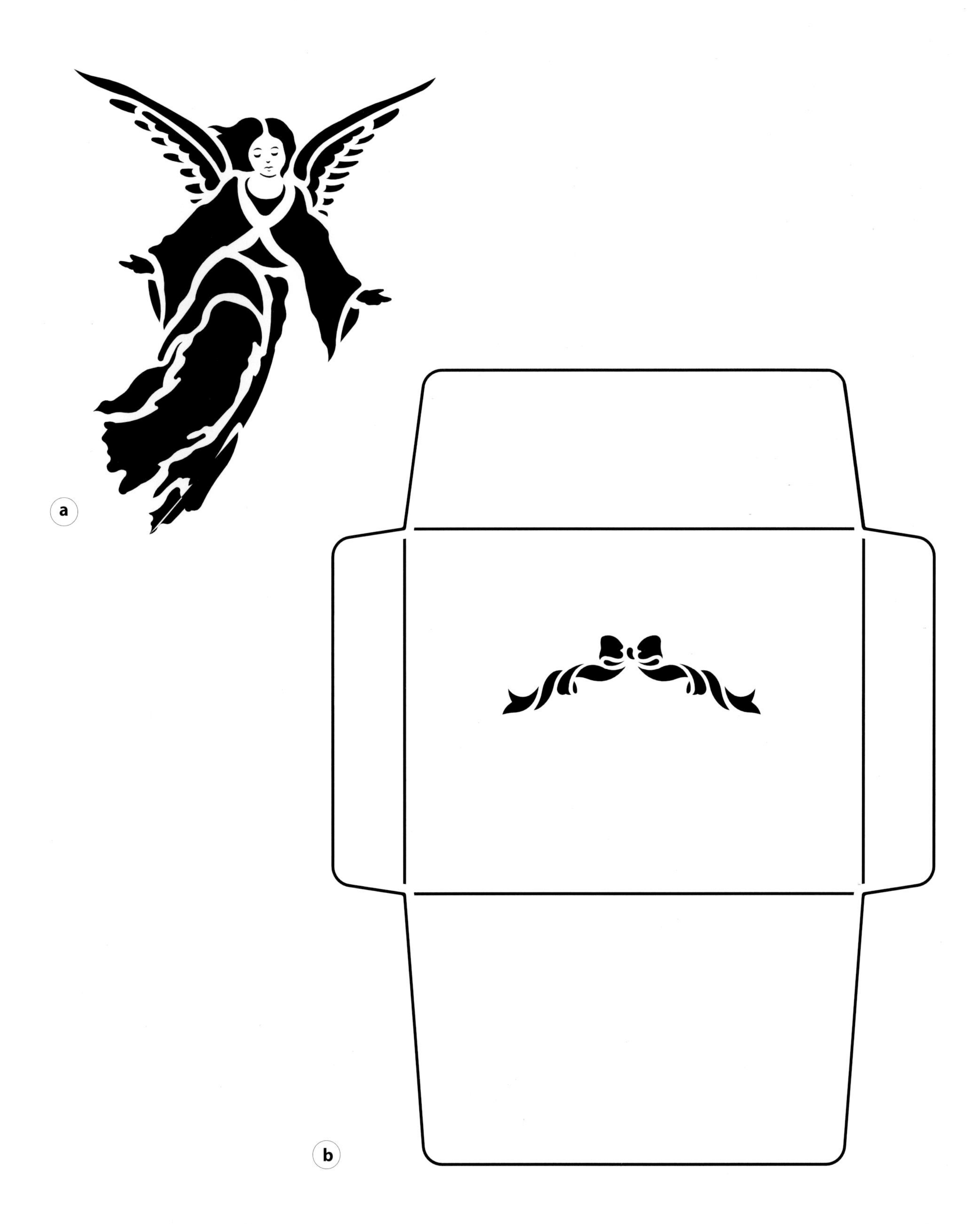

1 **Position stencil**

Position the angel stencil in the center of the small vellum sheet and attach with masking tape.

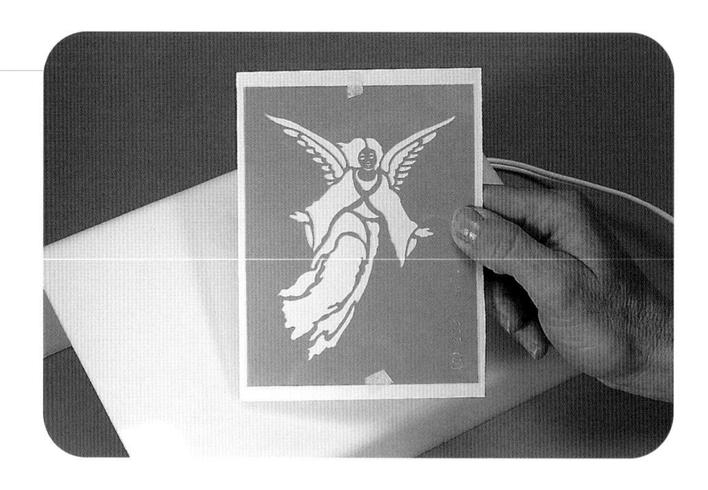

Emboss border 2

Flip stencil and vellum over and emboss around the edge of the stencil. (If you made your own stencil, cut it to 4" x 5" and emboss.)

3 **Emboss angel**

Emboss the angel. Remove stencil.

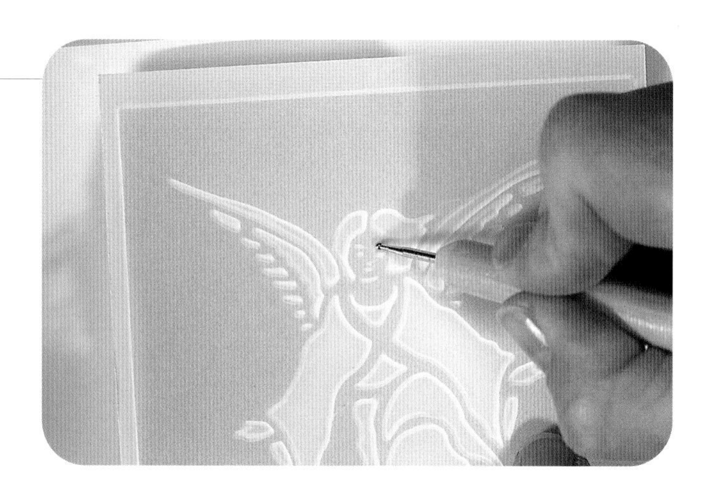

Trim vellum 4

Trim the vellum to the embossed border.

Paint background (5)

Turn the vellum over and use a brush and plain water to evenly moisten the paper around the angel. Using the watercolors, paint the background in random pastels up to the embossed angel. Thin colors with water to make them lighter, blotting the brush to prevent drips. You can paint on scrap paper to practice.

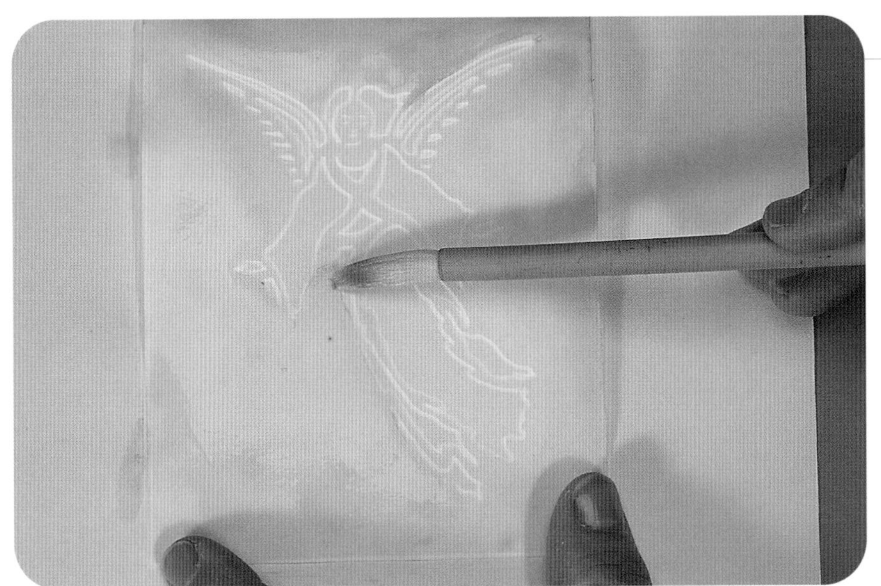

Finish background (6)

Once you have filled the background around the angel, paint lightly on the angel itself.

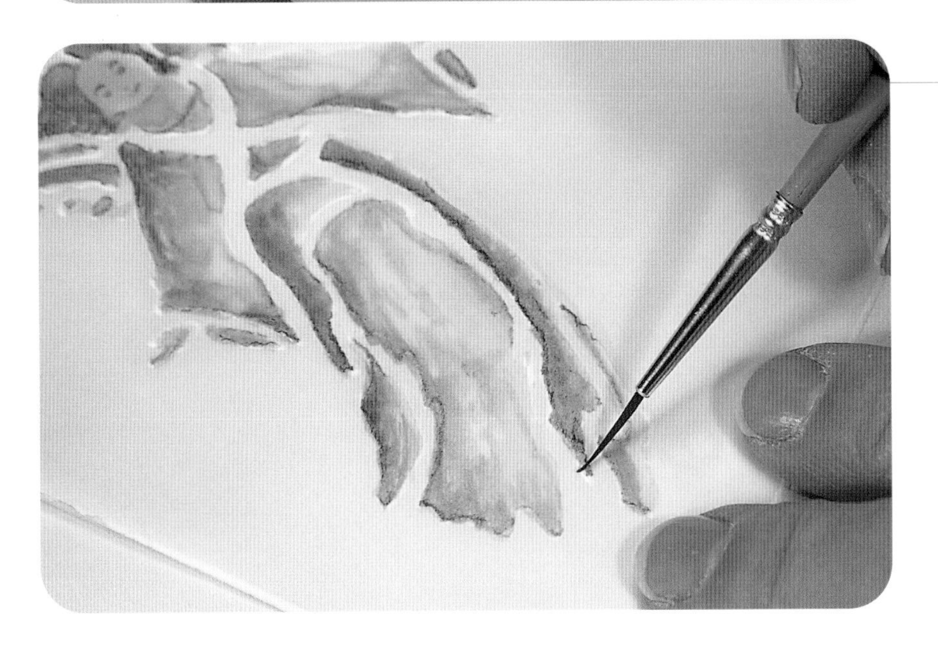

Paint the angel (7)

Turn the vellum over so the front side is up. Using the small watercolor brush, apply vibrant colors to the angel, staying within the embossed lines. To get a three-dimensional look, place the lightest colors in the center of each section and blend into the darkest colors at the edges.

8 Choose intense colors

The angel should be painted in more vibrant, intense colors against a muted pastel background.

9 Attach vellum to notecard

Apply glue stick to the back of the vellum, center the vellum on the front of the white notecard, and stick down.

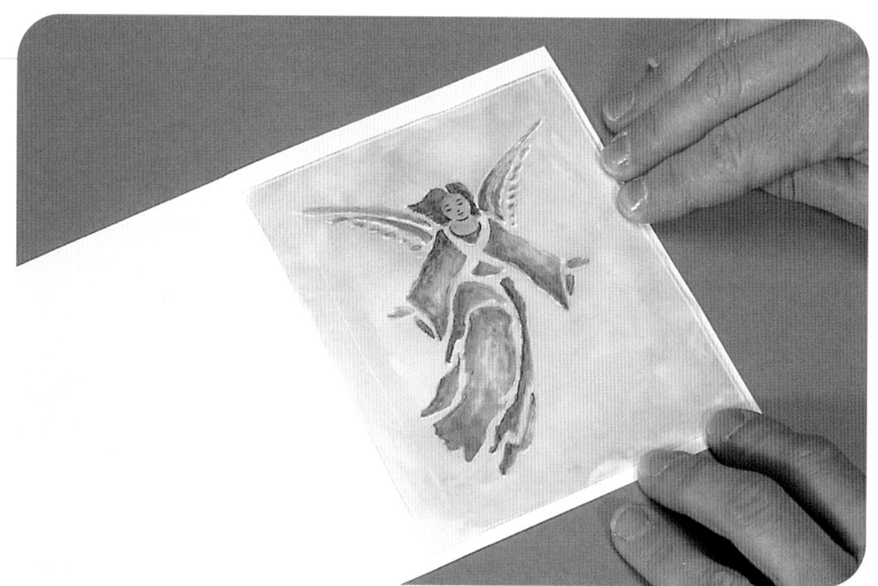

10 Attach liner

Glue the piece of lavender tissue on the inside left of the notecard. Press firmly to secure.

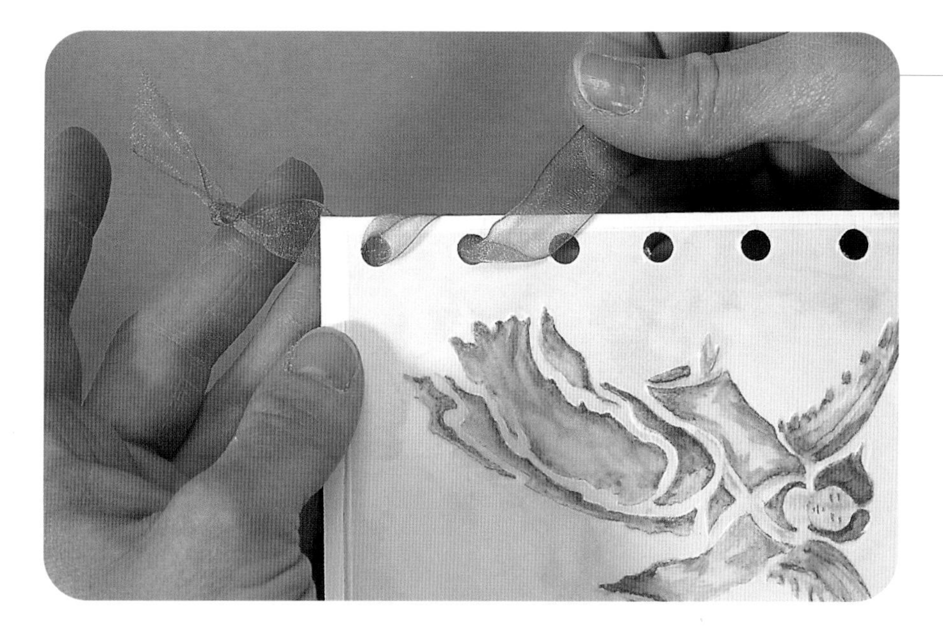

Add ribbon 11

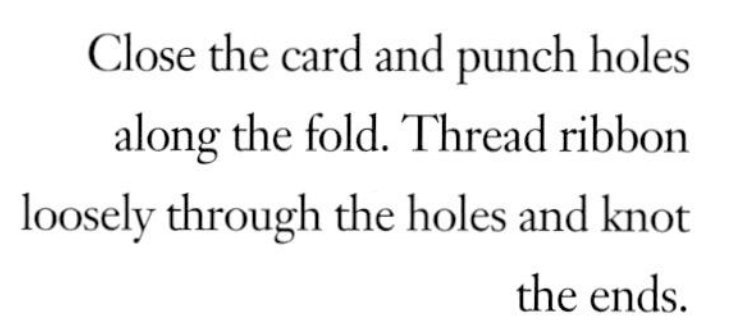

Close the card and punch holes along the fold. Thread ribbon loosely through the holes and knot the ends.

The finished card

12 Trace envelope template

Trace the envelope template onto the large sheet of white vellum. Do not transfer the ribbon pattern. Remove stencil and cut out the envelope.

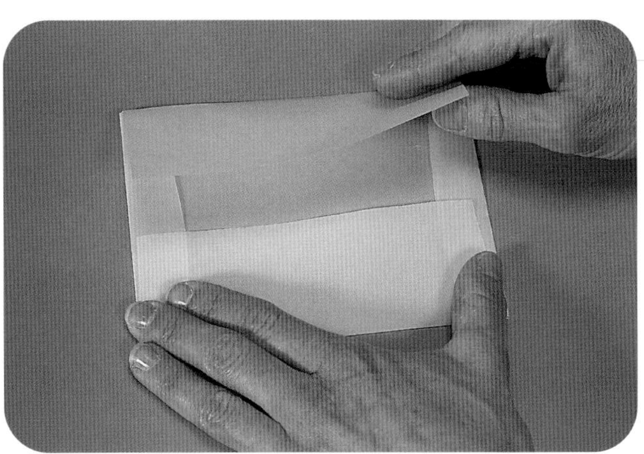

Fold envelope 13

Fold vellum along the lines to form the envelope.

14 Paint the vellum

Using a damp makeup sponge, sponge the vellum with random pastel watercolors.

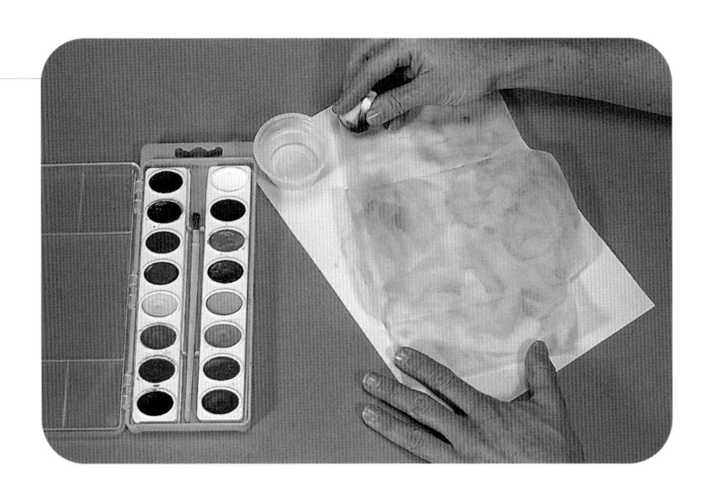

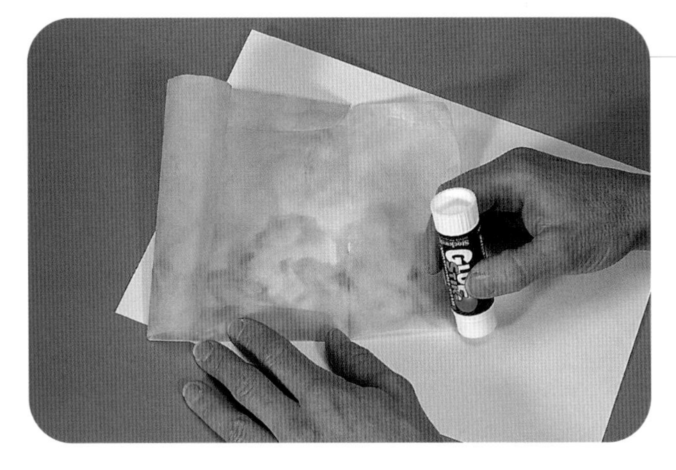

Glue envelope 15

Fold the sides of the envelope in first, then the bottom flap. Glue the edges, pressing firmly.

16 Add white envelope

Slide the white envelope that came with the card into the vellum envelope.

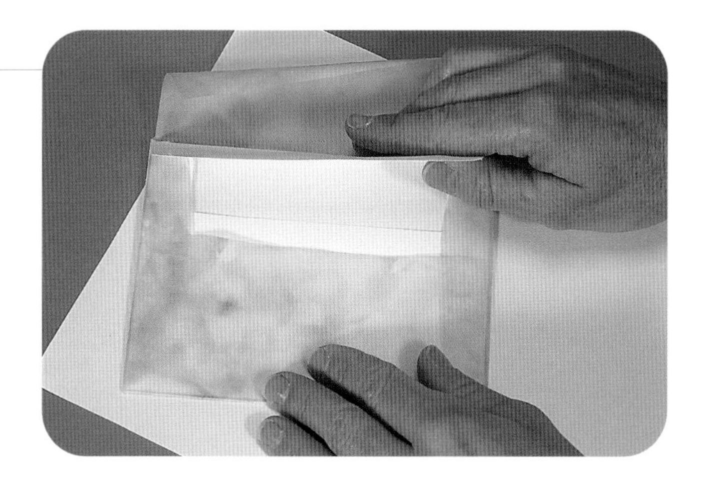

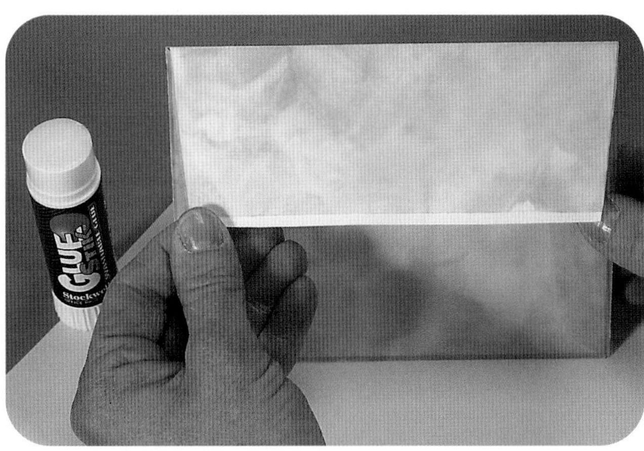

Glue envelopes together 17

Glue the vellum envelope flap to the white envelope flap. Trim as needed.

The finished card and envelope

Hummingbird Music Card

This card has a cozy feel because of the dried flower accents and antiquing on the sheet music. If your sheet music or photocopy looks too white, try dipping it in a glass of hot tea until it reaches the desired color. Press the wet sheet music between paper towels so it will dry flat.

Materials

- American Traditional stencil
  - FS-913 Hummingbird
- Paper
  - 3" x 4" white cardstock
  - 5½" x 4¼" ivory cardstock and envelope
  - sheet music (original or photocopy)
- Shiva Paintsticks
  - Azo Yellow
  - Burnt Umber
  - Naphthol Red
  - Ultramarine Blue
- 3/16" stencil brushes
- dried flowers
- embossing tool
- light box
- glue
- scissors
- wax paper

To make a stencil, photocopy this image at 50 percent and use a sharp craft knife to cut out the design. (a)

(a)

1 Position stencil

Center and tape stencil on the white cardstock.

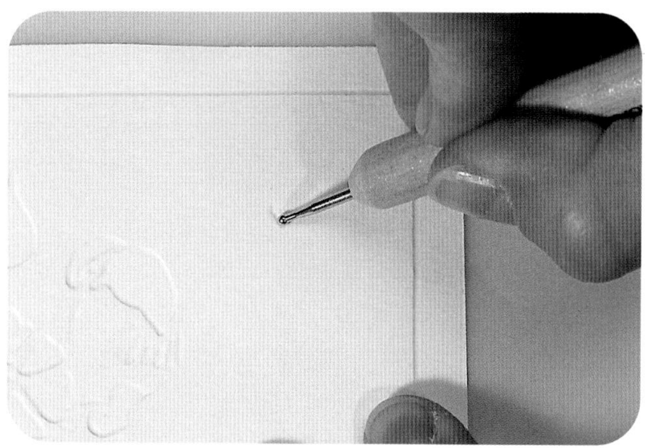

Emboss 2

Flip stencil and cardstock over and place on a light box. Emboss the border and complete image.

3 Stencil hummingbird

With stencil still in place, flip cardstock over and stencil the hummingbird and flowers with nicely blended yellow, red and blue oil stick colors (blend blue and yellow to make green; blue and red to make purple). Remove the stencil.

Cut out hummingbird 4

Cut out the stenciled image, following the outline of the raised embossed border.

5 Drybrush sky

Drybrush around the hummingbird with blue oil stick to create a sky.

Drybrush notecard 6

Reposition the hummingbird stencil over the stenciled image so that only the embossed border shows around the edges. Using the stencil as a mask, drybrush with Burnt Umber oil stick around the edge of the stencil to add color to the embossed border.

The finished hummingbird

7 Prepare sheet music

Tear the sheet music to form an irregular and interesting shape. Drybrush the edges with Burnt Umber to create an aged appearance.

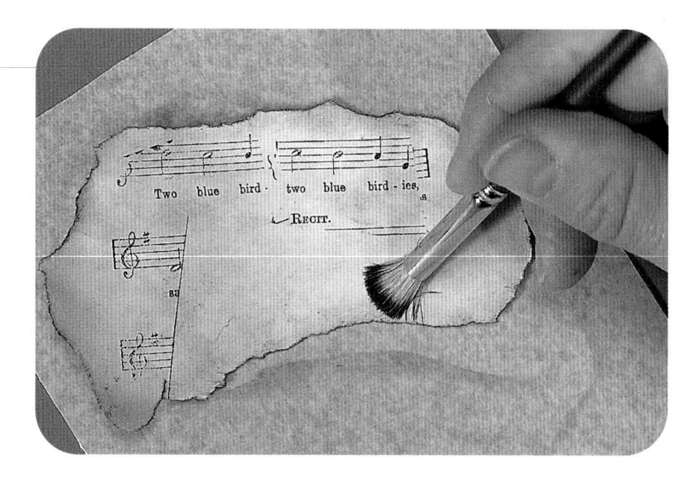

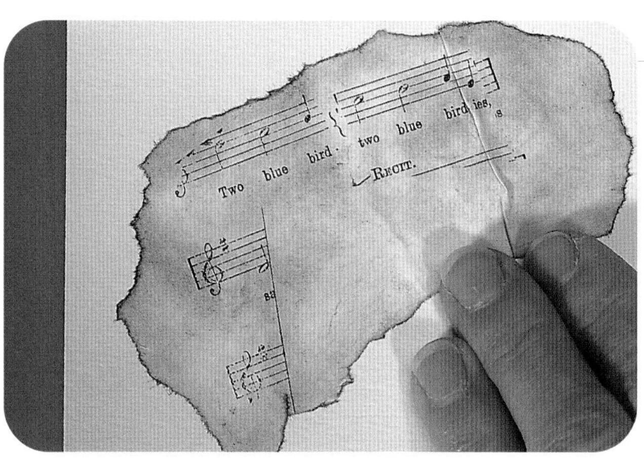

Glue music to card 8

Add glue to the back of the sheet music and spread glue to edges. Using the ivory cardstock, attach the sheet music to the card front, slightly off center and toward the upper left.

9 Add hummingbird

Glue the hummingbird card to the card front, overlapping the sheet music.

Add drybrushed color 10

Drybrush blue oil stick along the edges of card front. Then drybrush Burnt Umber near the sheet music and hummingbird.

11 Add flowers

Arrange and glue dried flowers in upper left and lower right corners.

The finished card

Sponged Vellum Tulip Card

When sponged together, the colors used for this card created a harmonious, muted effect. Choose your own color scheme according to the mood you want to convey: pale yellow, blue, pink and green for a springtime feel; white and grey sponging with bright tulips for a vibrant, zingy feel.

Materials

* American Traditional stencil
    * BL-13 Double Border
* Paper
    * 5½" x 4¼" ivory notecard with matching envelope
    * 5½" x 2" sheet of white vellum
* DecoArt Americana acrylic paints
    * Base Flesh
    * Brandy Wine
    * Wedgewood Blue
* clear embossing powder
* 3/16" stencil brushes
* embossing tool
* light box
* heat gun
* Fiskars Victorian decorative edging scissors
* toothbrush
* glue
* sea sponge or similar sponge
* bookmark tassel
* small container of water
* wax paper
* foam plate
* masking tape

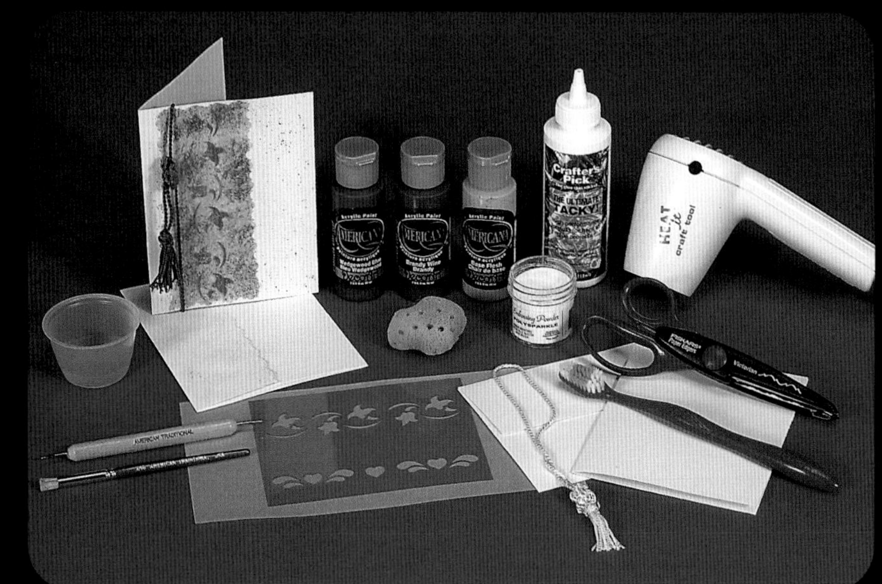

To make a stencil, photocopy this image at 67 percent and use a sharp craft knife to cut out the design. 

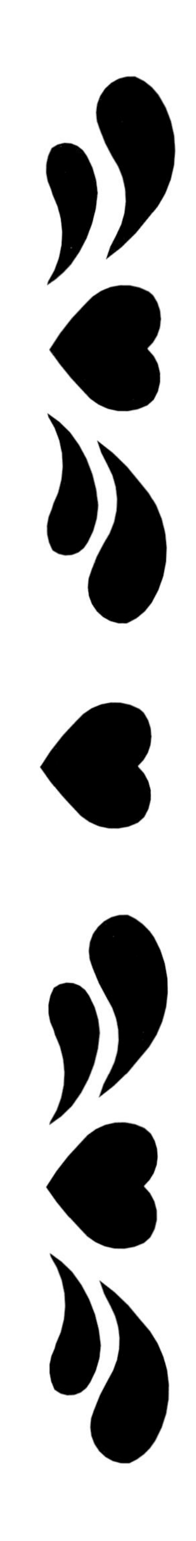

a

1 Trim vellum

Trim the vellum with the decorative edging scissors.

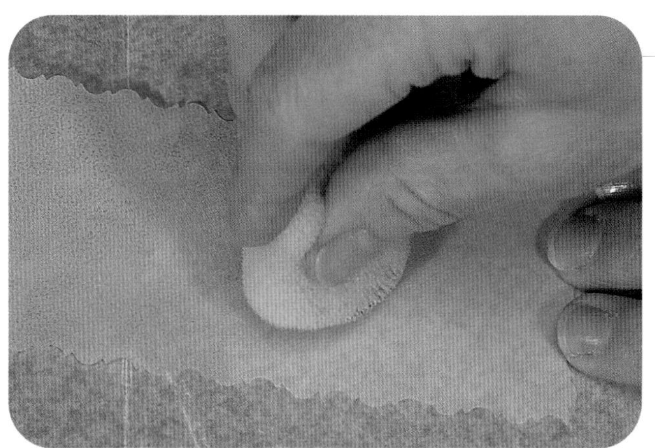

Sponge Base Flesh 2

Squeeze a small amount of each paint color onto the foam plate. Dip the sea sponge in water and wring it out. Then dip it in Base Flesh and dab off the excess. Sponge Base Flesh over vellum, allowing sponge texture to show.

3 Sponge Brandy Wine

Repeat the sponging process with Brandy Wine, allowing some Base Flesh to show through.

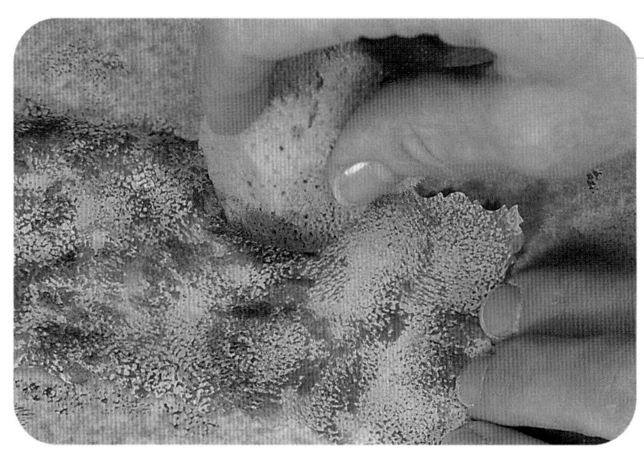

Sponge Wedgewood Blue 4

Repeat sponging with Wedgewood Blue, making sure the blue is consistent over the vellum but that Base Flesh and Brandy Wine colors still show through. Allow to dry (the paint will dry quickly).

5 Position stencil

Center the tulip pattern of the stencil over the vellum and tape in place.

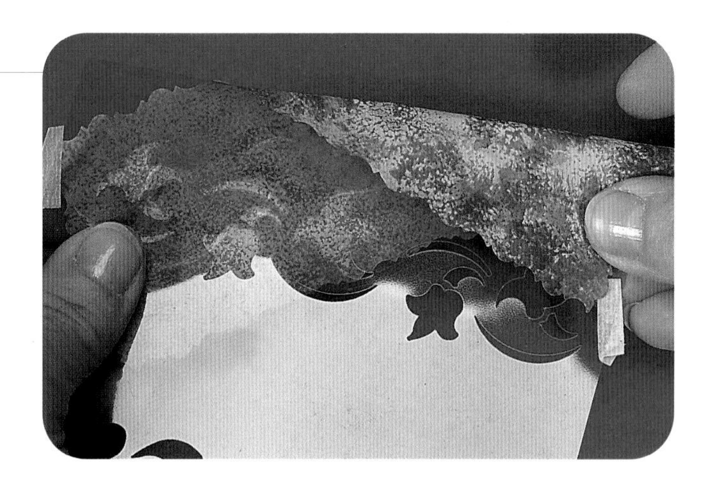

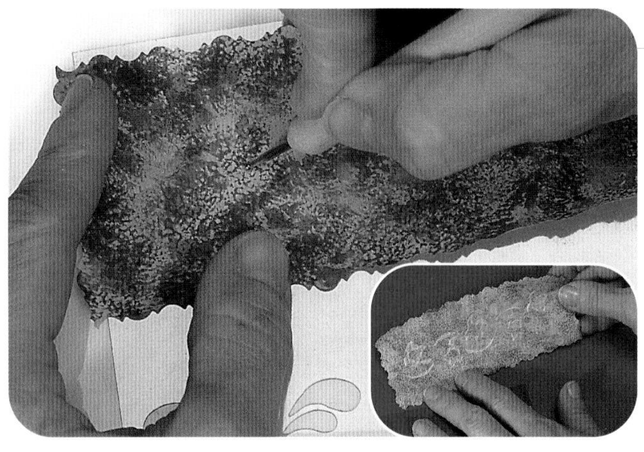

Emboss 6

Flip stencil and vellum over onto a light box. Emboss the tulip pattern.

7 Stencil tulip pattern

Flip the vellum over to the front and stencil the tulip pattern in Brandy Wine.

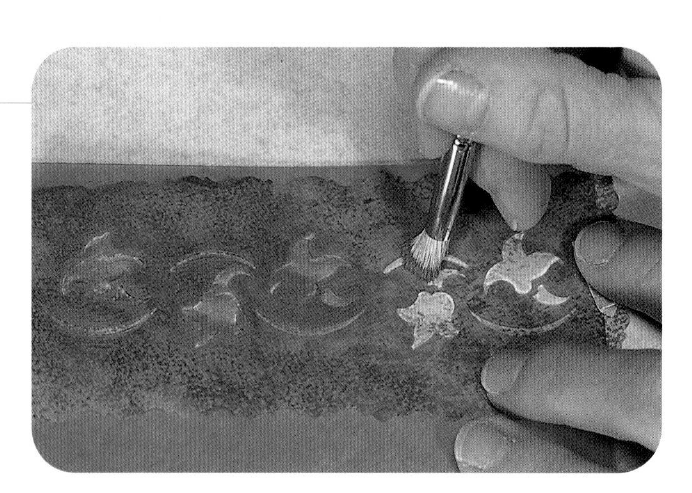

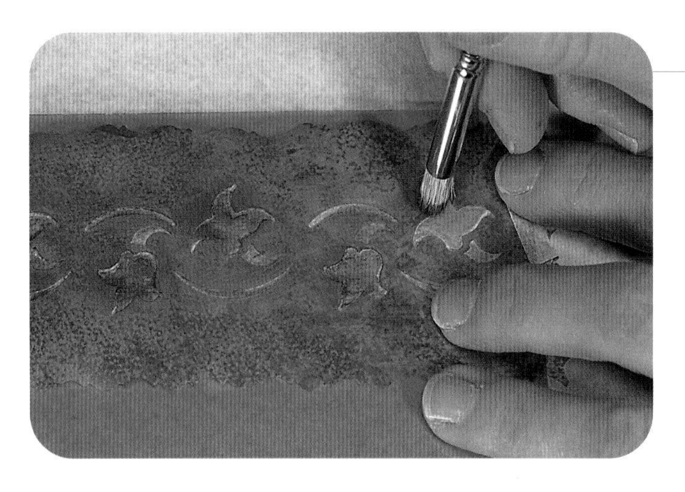

Add Wedgewood Blue 8

Stencil again in Wedgewood Blue, allowing the red and blue to mix in places but preserving some mottled color.

9 Add glue

Squeeze a small amount of glue onto the foam plate. Stencil a final layer of glue into the tulip pattern. Remove the stencil.

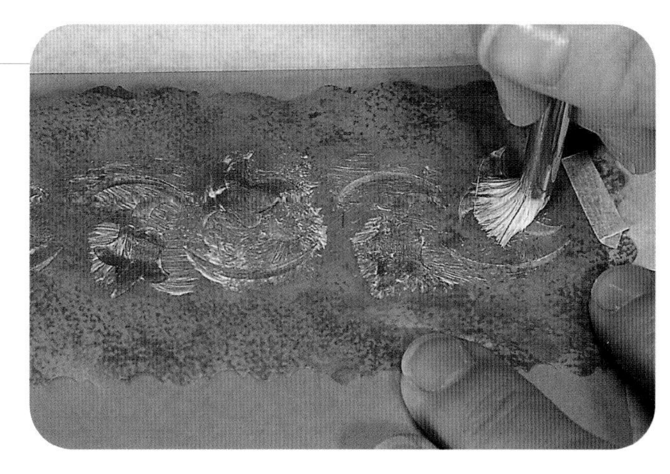

Add embossing powder 10

While the glue is still wet, pour clear embossing powder over the design. Shake off the excess.

11 Heat

Heat the embossing powder until it melts.

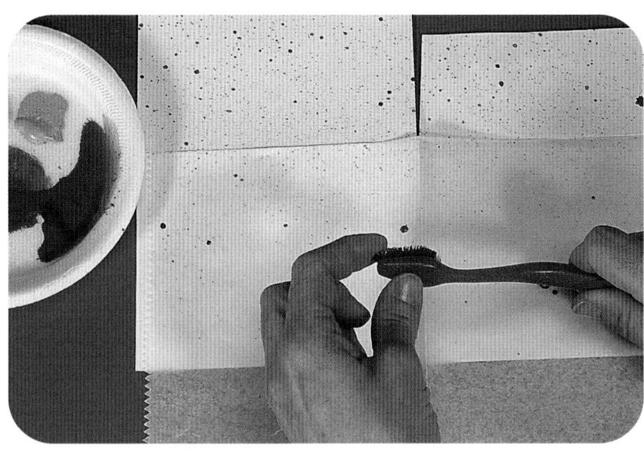

Spatter card background 12

Open the notecard onto a sheet of wax paper so the front faces away from you. Place the envelope face up and with the flap out. Protect the back of the notecard and the front of the envelope with wax paper. Dip the toothbrush in water, blot on paper towel, and dip into Brandy Wine paint. Tap off the excess. Scrape your finger across the bristles to spatter paint on the card front and envelope flap.

13 Trim envelope flap

Trim the envelope flap with the decorative edging scissors.

Attach vellum to card 14

Apply glue to the back of the vellum and attach it to the front of the card approximately ¼-inch from the fold.

15 Add tassel

Slide the tassel over the card until it is positioned in the fold so that the tassel hangs on the outside of the card. Adjust length if necessary.

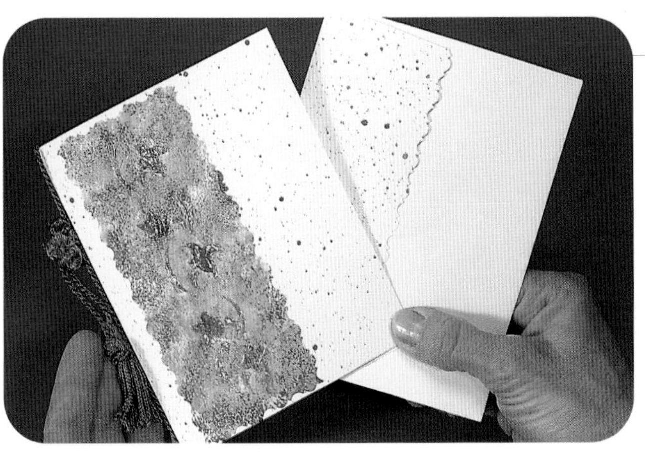

The finished card and envelope 

Cutting and Piercing

Get out a fresh blade for your craft knife! You'll use it in these projects to create decorative cutouts, pierced paper and paper tole, a three-dimensional layered effect. Cutouts can be backed with contrasting paper or used as photo frames for those special snapshots you just have to share. Paper piercing adds depth, interest and elegance to your design. Paper tole is a way of layering elements of your design to create what is almost a paper sculpture. You may just want to frame the card for yourself when you're done! You'll soon see how the techniques in this chapter can be applied to many different designs.

Cutout Teapot Notecard

This colorful teapot is embossed, stenciled, cut out and backed with contrasting paper to form an eye-catching design. Who would be able to guess that you made it yourself? This technique can be adapted to any design, as long as the stenciled image has enough contact points with the border to keep the stenciling attached to the card.

Materials

- American Traditional stencil
  - GS-132 Posh Tea Pot
- Paper
  - 5½" x 4¼" white notecard with matching envelope
  - 5½" x 4¼" cranberry handmade mulberry paper
- Shiva Paintstiks
  - Azo Yellow
  - Naphthol Red
  - Prussian Blue
  - Sap Green
- 3/16" stencil brushes
- embossing tool
- light box
- Fiskars scallop decorative edging scissors
- Zig 2-Way glue
- craft knife
- wax paper
- masking tape

To make a stencil, photocopy this image at 50 percent and use a sharp craft knife to cut out the design. (a)

(a)

1 Position stencil

Position stencil on center front of white notecard and tape in place.

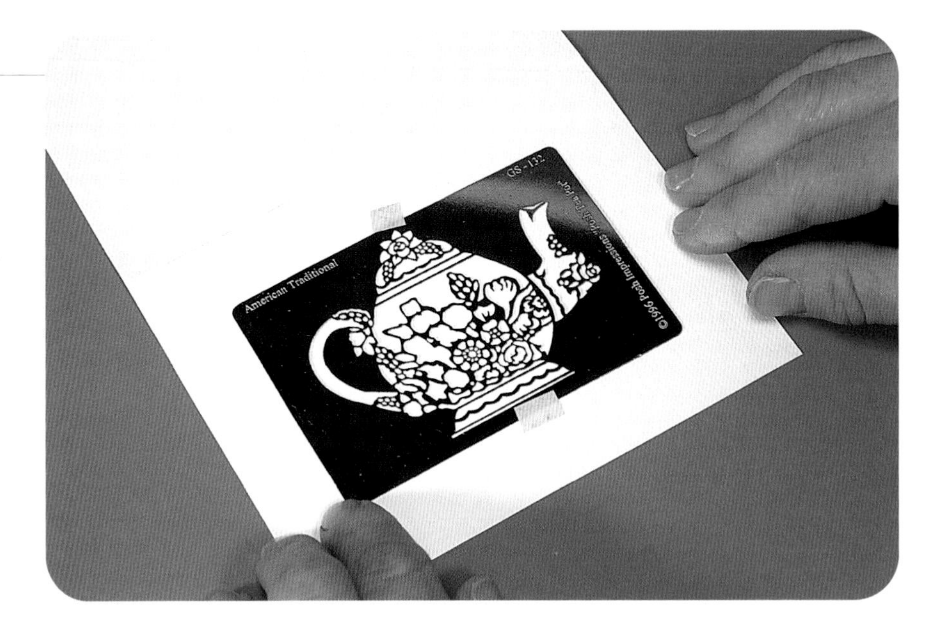

2 Emboss border

Flip paper and stencil over onto a light box. After rubbing your fingers across the area to be embossed to make the tool slide more easily, trace along the outside edge of the stencil to form a border.

3 Stencil teapot

Flip paper and stencil to front and stencil the teapot with oil sticks in the colors of your choice.

Cut out teapot background 4

With a sharp craft knife, cut around the teapot inside of the embossed border, leaving the teapot attached to the card at the top, spout, handle and base. You may want to slip a piece of glass or cardboard under the notecard as you're cutting.

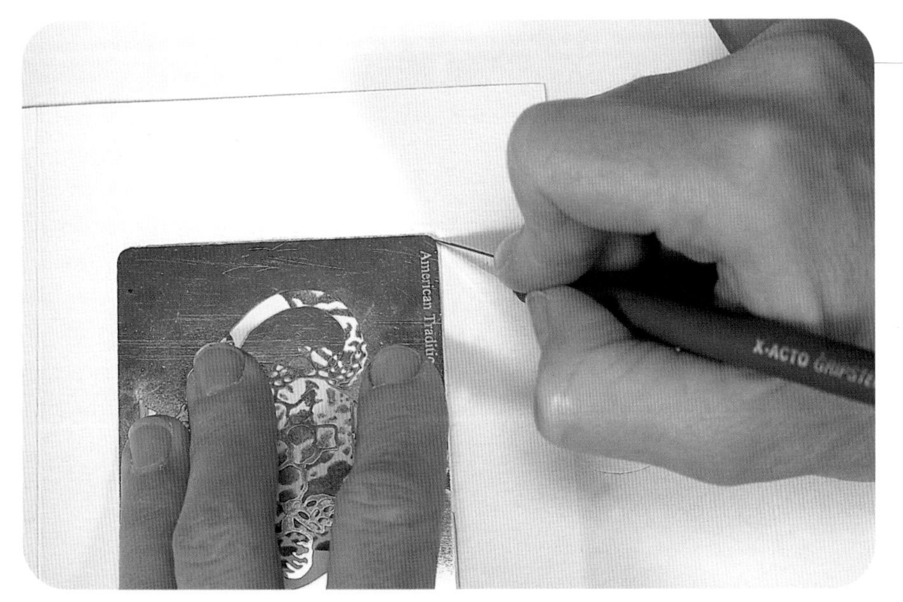

Use the stencil border as a guide 5

To make straight edges and perfect corners, use the stencil as a cutting guide around the border.

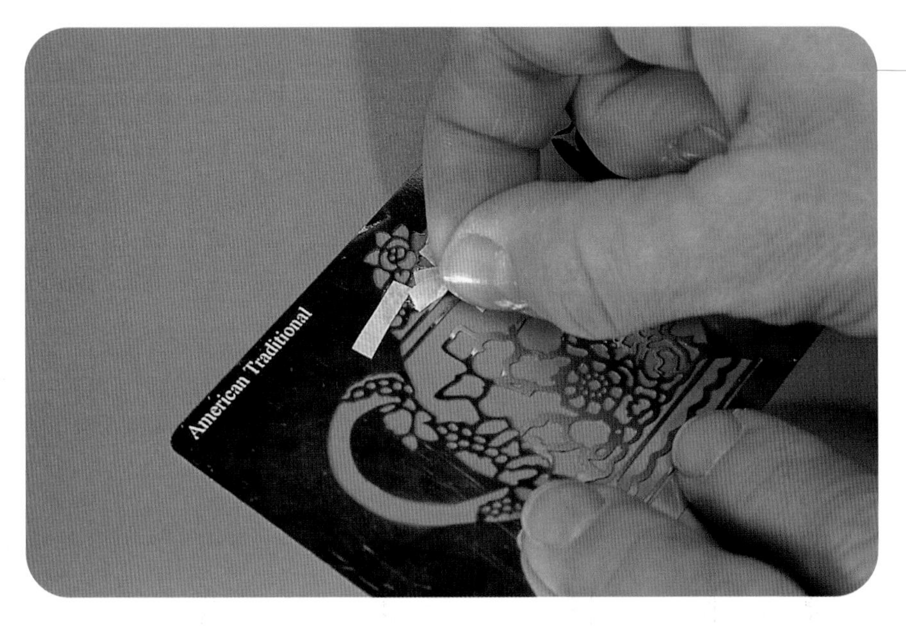

Mask off flower 6

Use masking tape to shield off the flower at the top of the teapot. This will make it easier to stencil just the flower design.

7 Emboss and stencil flower

Emboss and stencil the flower in a few places around the edges of the card. Use red, yellow and blue and mixtures of these colors.

8 Attach contrasting paper

Apply glue to the edges of the handmade paper. Secure the paper to the inside of the card on the left side, behind the teapot.

9 Drybrush border

Using red oil stick, drybrush a ¼" border on the bottom inside edge of the card. Use the straight edge of scrap or wax paper as a guide.

Edge card front (10)

Trim the bottom edge of the card front with decorative edging scissors.

The finished card

Cut-and-Pierce Tulip Wreath Photo Card

Do you have a snapshot that you can't wait to share? This card is a great way to do it. Not only is the card an elegant presentation device, but it can be used by the recipient as a frame for display.

Materials

- American Traditional stencils
  - BL-72 Oval Frame
  - BL-31 Triple Border
- Paper
  - 5½" x 4¼" white notecard and envelope
  - 5½" x 4¼" cranberry handmade mulberry paper
- Sakura Cray-Pas oil pastels in pink and green
- 3" x 5" photograph
- 3/16" stencil brushes
- embossing tool
- light box
- craft knife
- glue
- wax paper
- masking tape

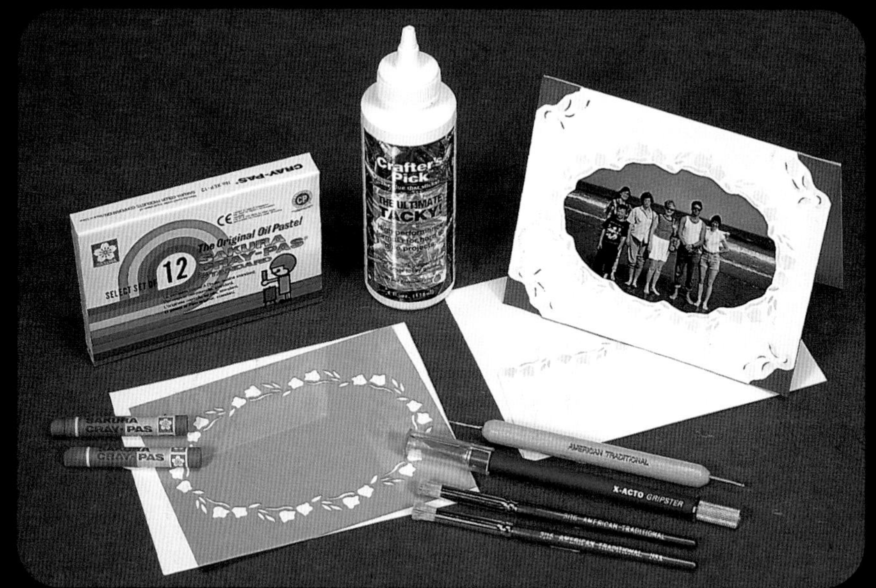

BL-72. To make a stencil, photocopy this image at 100 percent and use a sharp craft knife to cut out the design. **a**

BL-31. To make a stencil, photocopy this image at 100 percent and use a sharp craft knife to cut out the design. **b**

a

b

1 Create palette

Wax paper makes an excellent palette for oil pastels. Rub smears of each color onto your palette.

2 Emboss Oval Frame

Use tape to attach the Oval Frame stencil to center of notecard front. Flip over on light box and emboss.

3 Stencil Oval Frame

Flip the notecard back to the front and stencil with the pink and green oil pastels.

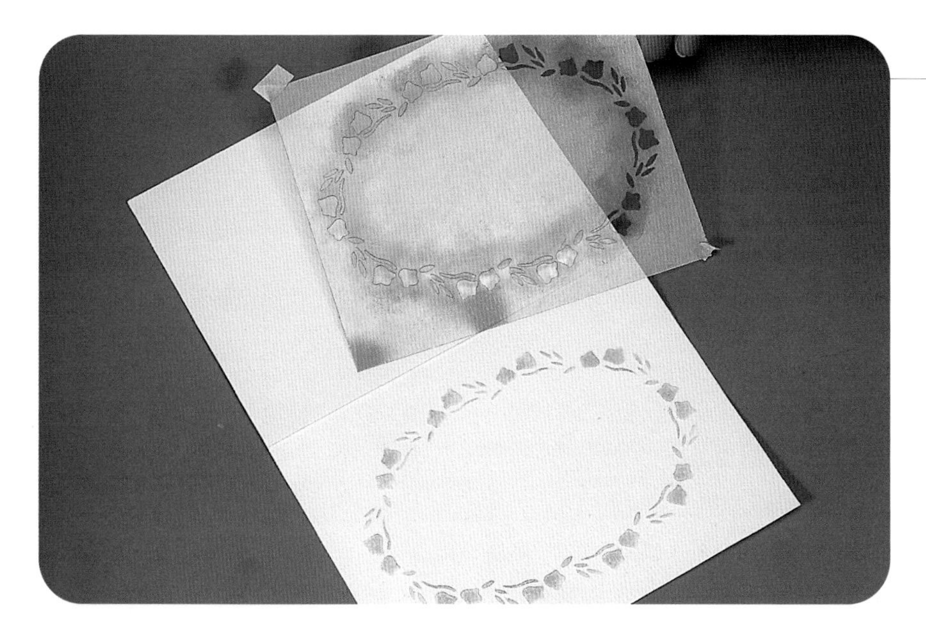

Remove stencil 4

Emboss and stencil tulips 5

Position a tulip design from the border stencil in a corner of the card front. Emboss and stencil using red, yellow, blue and mixtures of those colors. Repeat in all corners.

Trim corners and cut frame 6

Use a craft knife to trim all four corners following the tulip design. Cut two straight edges at fold of card and connect the cutout in upper corners as shown. Cut out the center oval by following the tulip wreath pattern. Slip cardboard, glass, or a cutting mat under the card before you start cutting.

7 Cut and pierce

Transform the tulip corners into "cut-and-pierce" designs by making small slices with a craft knife along one side of the buds and leaves.

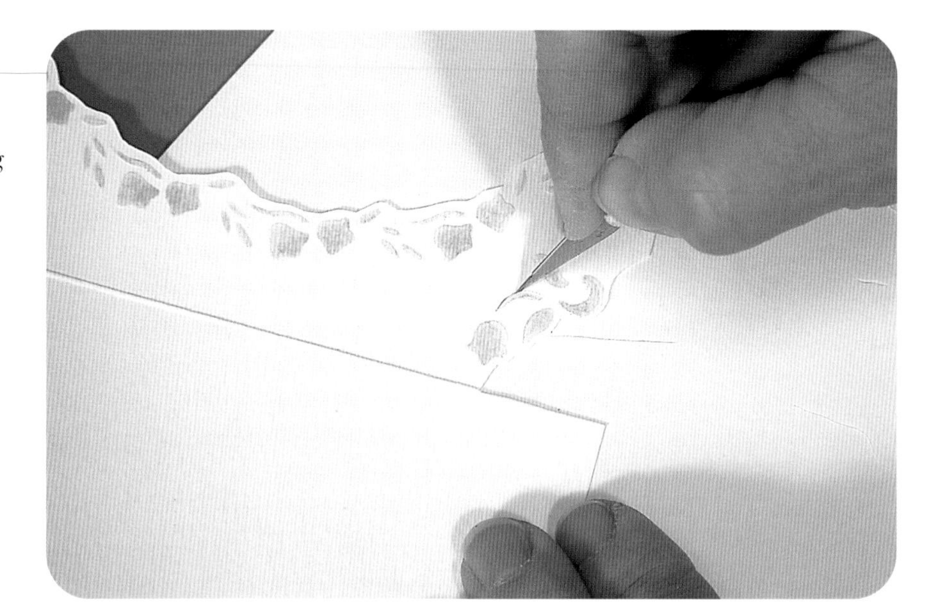

8 Glue photo in frame

Apply glue to the back of the oval opening in the wreath frame. Center the photo in the frame, trimming edges if necessary. Press firmly to secure.

9 Glue in backing

Apply more glue to the back of the photo and the edges of the card. Affix the contrasting handmade paper, trimmed to the original size of the notecard.

Decorate envelope 

Stencil an envelope to match the card.

Paper Tole Tulip

Paper tole is a process by which several identical images are cut and layered to create a three-dimensional paper sculpture. This paper tole tulip makes an impressive card that can be framed and hung as a piece of art.

Materials

- American Traditional stencil
    - CS-21 Three-Part Tulip
- Paper
    - 5½" x 4¼" white, ivory or beige notecard with matching envelope
    - 8½" x 11" white cardstock
- Shiva Paintstiks
    - Azo Yellow
    - Naphthol Red
    - Ultramarine Blue
- DecoArt Americana acrylic paint in Black Green
- three ³⁄₁₆" stencil brushes
- craft knife or small straight scissors
- double-sided foam tape
- toothbrush
- wax paper
- masking tape

CS-21 Part 1. To make a stencil, photocopy this image at 133 percent and use a sharp craft knife to cut out the design. **a**

CS-21 Part 2. To make a stencil, photocopy this image at 133 percent and use a sharp craft knife to cut out the design. **b**

CS-21 Part 3. To make a stencil, photocopy this image at 133 percent and use a sharp craft knife to cut out the design. **c**

1 Spatter card

Open the notecard and place on scrap paper facing up. Speckle the background by putting a small amount of Black Green acrylic paint on a toothbrush, tapping onto paper towel, then flicking bristles with fingers.

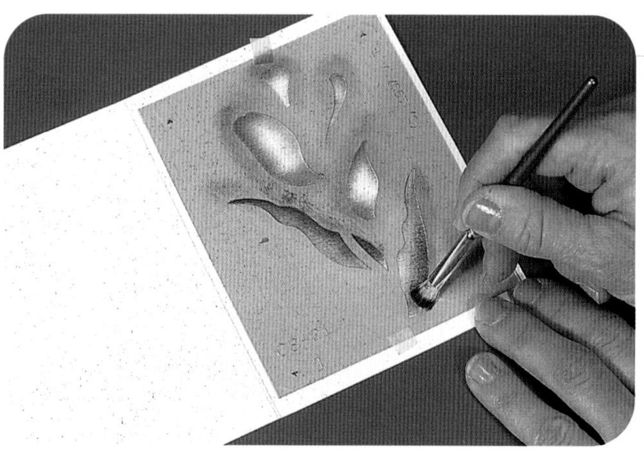

Stencil tulip 2

Center and attach part 1 of the tulip stencil on the front of the notecard. Trace registration marks. Use oil stick colors to stencil all three parts of the tulip, mixing Azo Yellow and Ultramarine Blue for varying shades of green. Control your shades of pink by using more or less red. See the images on page 95 for a color guide.

3 Repeat stenciling

Stencil the tulip four more times on the 8½" x 11" sheet of cardstock.

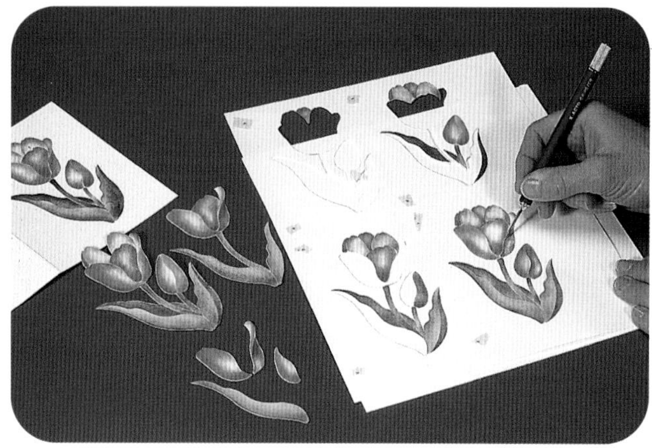

Cut tulip layers 4

Using small sharp scissors or a craft knife, cut the parts of the tulip for the four layers. See the guide on page 95 for which elements to cut for each layer. You will layer the tulip elements from back to front, with the parts that would be furthest away from the viewer in the back. This creates a three-dimensional effect.

5 Add foam tape

Cut ⅛" x ¼" pieces of double-sided foam tape and mount the pieces on the back of the tulip elements. As you add each layer, peel the protective layer off the foam tape. You will need about twenty-four pieces of foam tape. Use as many pieces as necessary to hold each element of the design securely in place.

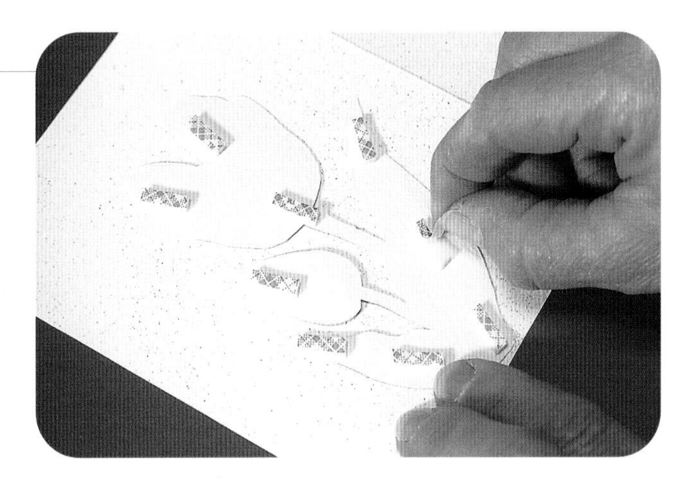

Add first layer 6

Place the first layer on top of the stenciled tulip on card front. This layer is the whole pattern, less one small tulip petal in background.

7 Add second layer

Repeat with the second layer, aligning the tulips exactly on top of one another.

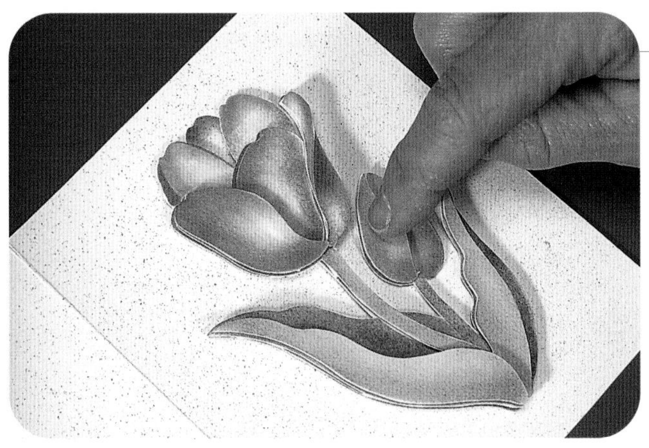

Add third layer 8

9 Add fourth and final layer

The finished card

The finished card makes a lovely framed piece.

1. The dotted lines indicate which sections to cut for the first (bottom) layer.

2. The dotted lines indicate which sections to cut for the second layer.

3. The dotted lines indicate which sections to cut for the third layer.

4. The dotted lines indicate which sections to cut for the fourth (top) layer.

Merry Christmas
Have a Beary Happy Birthday

Special Effects

Some of the preceding projects have used special materials such as glitter and embossing powder. Here are some more projects that use nontraditional materials—including foil, polymer clay, shrink plastic and a woodburning tool—for creating special effects with your stencils.

Foil Ornament Card

In addition to glitter and embossing powder, you can use foil to add shine to your stenciled greeting cards. Look for foil in your local art and craft supply store. I've chosen Crafter's Pick, The Ultimate Tacky! glue for this project, but you can also use any quick-drying foil glue.

Materials

- American Traditional stencil
  BL-79 Ornaments
- Paper
  5½" x 4¼" white notecard with matching envelope
- gold foil
- Crafter's Pick, The Ultimate Tacky! glue or other suitable glue
- 3/16" stencil brushes
- embossing tool
- light-colored glitter
- heat gun or hair dryer (optional)
- wax paper
- Fiskars rounder decorative edging scissors (optional)
- 12" length of 1/8"-wide holographic ribbon
- masking tape

BL-79. To make a stencil, photocopy this image at 53 percent and use a sharp craft knife to cut out the design. (a)

1 Stencil with glue

Place a small amount of glue on wax paper. Position stencil on notecard and secure with tape. Stencil notecard using glue instead of paint. Allow to dry thoroughly. A heat gun or hair dryer may be used to speed drying. Carefully remove stencil.

2 Apply foil

Lay foil over glue image, gold side facing up.

3 Burnish

Thoroughly burnish foil onto card with the flat side of the embossing tool, pressing firmly.

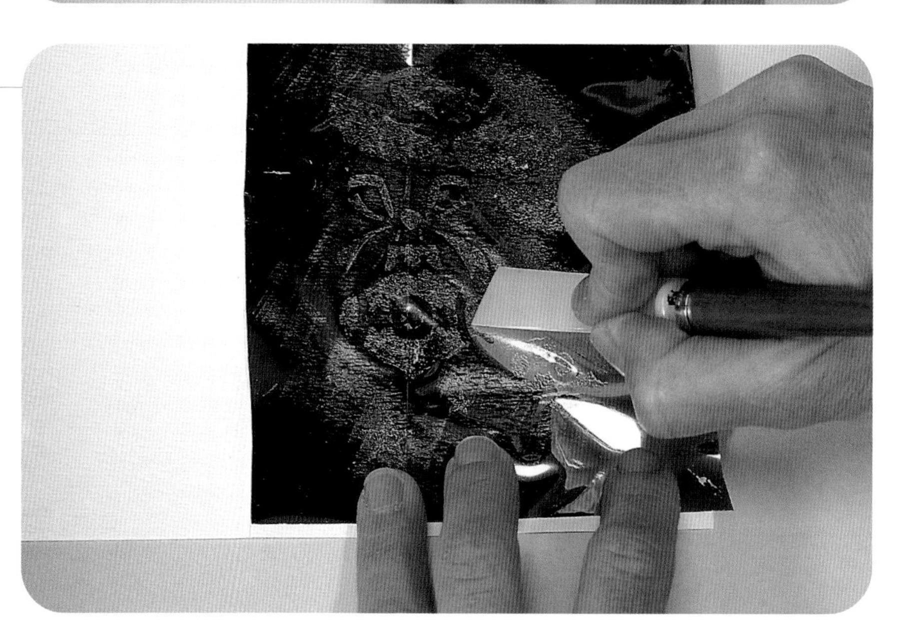

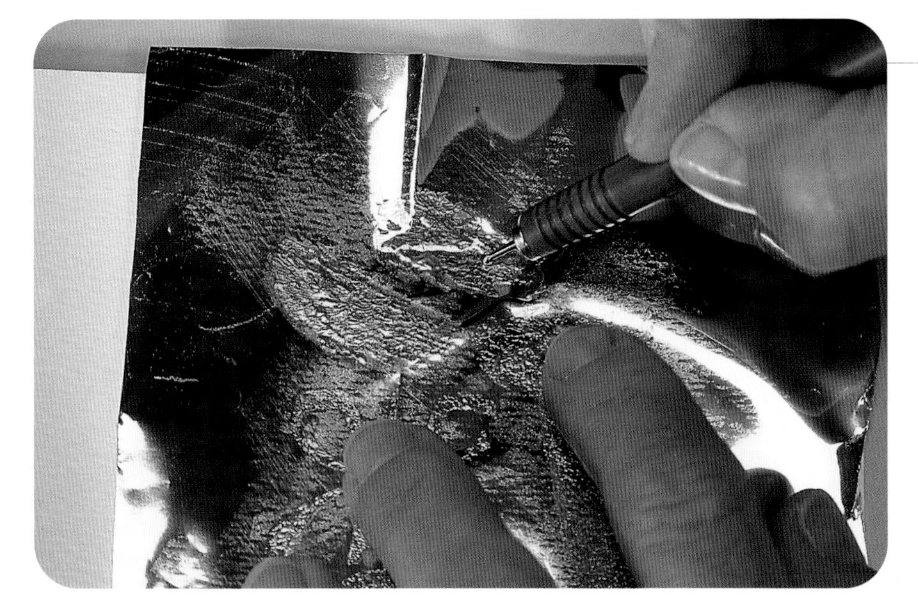

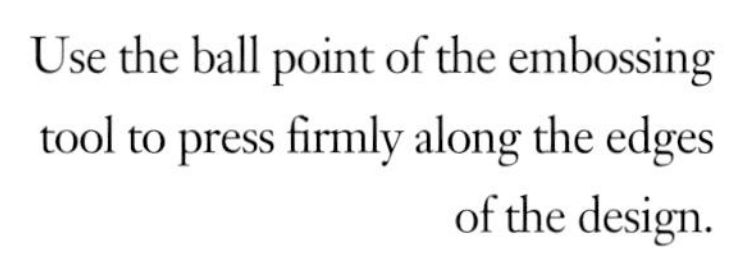

Burnish edges 4

Use the ball point of the embossing tool to press firmly along the edges of the design.

Remove foil 

Gently peel away the foil. Only the foil transferred to the ornaments should remain.

Remove excess foil 

Remove any out-of-place specks of foil with masking tape.

7 Add dots of glue

For extra sparkles, apply dots of glue where desired using the tip of the embossing tool.

8 Add glitter

Sprinkle glitter onto the glue, shaking off the excess.

9 Add ribbon

If you wish, use corner rounders or regular scissors to round the card corners. Wrap holographic ribbon around middle of the card at the fold and tie.

Double-Embossed Glossy Leaves

Double layers of embossing powder can create dramatic effects. Use these leaves to decorate your cards or other craft projects.

Materials

- American Traditional stencil
  - GS-136 Falling Leaves
- Paper
  - 3" x 3" white cardstock
- Shiva Paintstiks
  - Azo Yellow
  - Naphthol Red
- 3/16" stencil brushes
- Zig 2-Way glue
- Clear embossing powder
- Black embossing powder
- heat gun
- wax paper
- craft knife or scissors

To make a stencil, photocopy this image at 50 percent and use a sharp craft knife to cut out the design. 

1 Make leaf base

Start by stenciling a leaf with mixtures of yellow and red. Sprinkle with clear embossing powder, shaking off excess powder. Heat to melt. Cut out the leaf. Next, outline veins on the leaf with glue.

2 Add black embossing powder

Sprinkle black embossing powder over the wet glue.

3 Shake off excess

Heat  4

Use the heat gun to melt the powder.

The finished leaf 

Apply the finished leaf to cards or other craft projects.

Clay and Crinkle Sun Card

Here is a truly unique use for your stencils. When a stencil is run through a pasta roller with polymer clay, the stencil embosses the clay. Cut the design from the clay, and you have a work of art!

Materials

- American Traditional stencils
  - FS-918 Sun
  - MS-210 Grapes & Scroll
- Paper
  - $5\frac{1}{2}$" x $8\frac{1}{2}$" beige or tan cardstock folded to $5\frac{1}{2}$" x $4\frac{1}{4}$"
  - 2"x 8" green paper
  - 2"x 4" beige paper
- Shiva Oilstick in Sap Green
- Premo! polymer clay in Gold
- $\frac{3}{16}$" stencil brushes
- embossing tool
- pasta roller
- Fiskars paper crimper
- light box
- craft knife
- glue (such as Crafter's Pick, The Ultimate Tacky!)
- gold glitter (optional)
- heat gun or hair dryer (optional)
- wax paper
- masking tape
- scissors

FS-918. To make a stencil, photocopy this image at 55 percent and use a sharp craft knife to cut out the design. **a**

MS-210. To make a stencil, photocopy this image at 50 percent and use a sharp craft knife to cut out the design. **b**

a

b

1 Flatten polymer clay

Use your palm to flatten a 1-inch cube of gold clay. Place the clay in the pasta roller and roll it into a ⅛-inch-thick sheet.

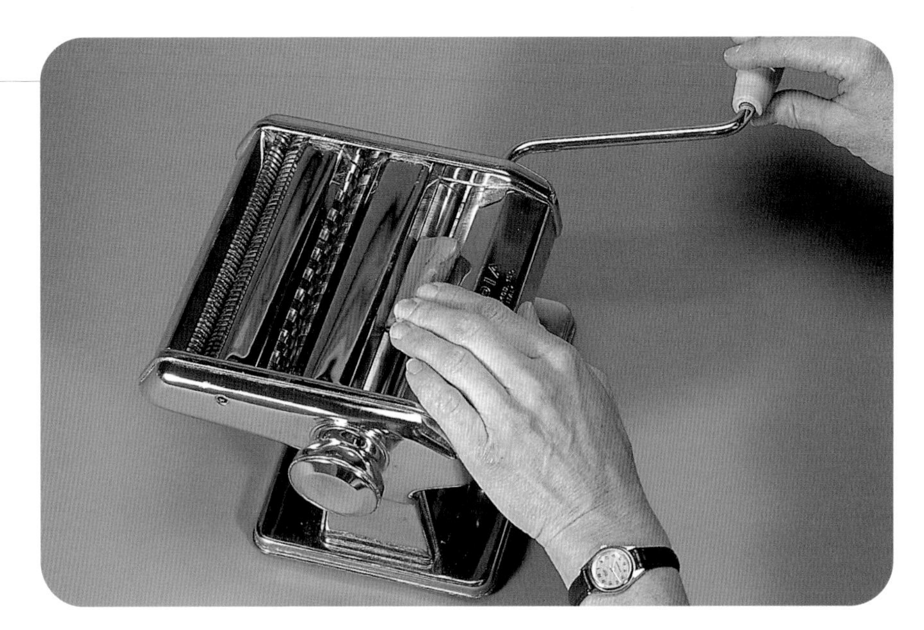

2 Roll clay with stencil

Place the sun stencil on the flattened clay and run them both through the pasta roller.

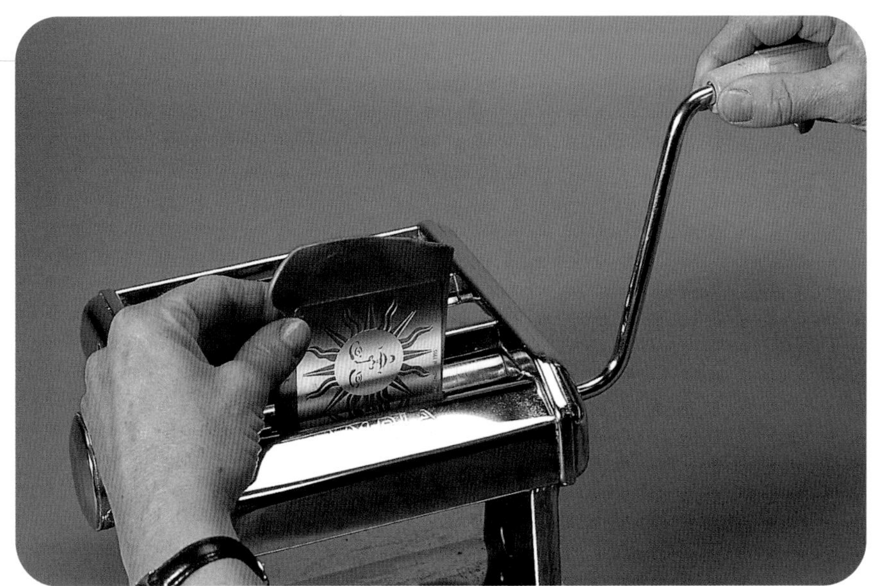

3 Remove stencil

Carefully remove the stencil from the clay to reveal an embossed image of the stencil.

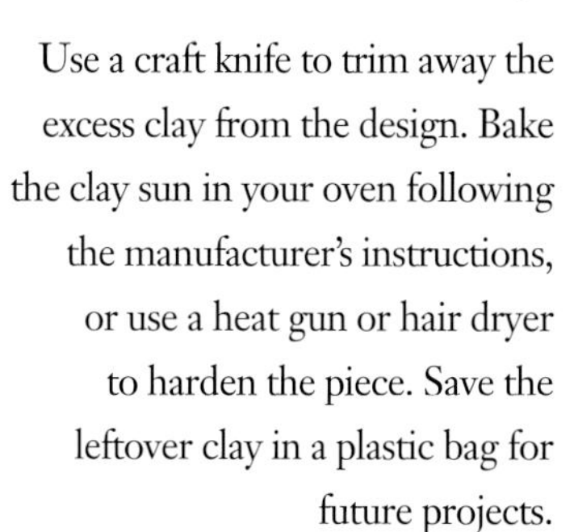

Cut out design 4

Use a craft knife to trim away the excess clay from the design. Bake the clay sun in your oven following the manufacturer's instructions, or use a heat gun or hair dryer to harden the piece. Save the leftover clay in a plastic bag for future projects.

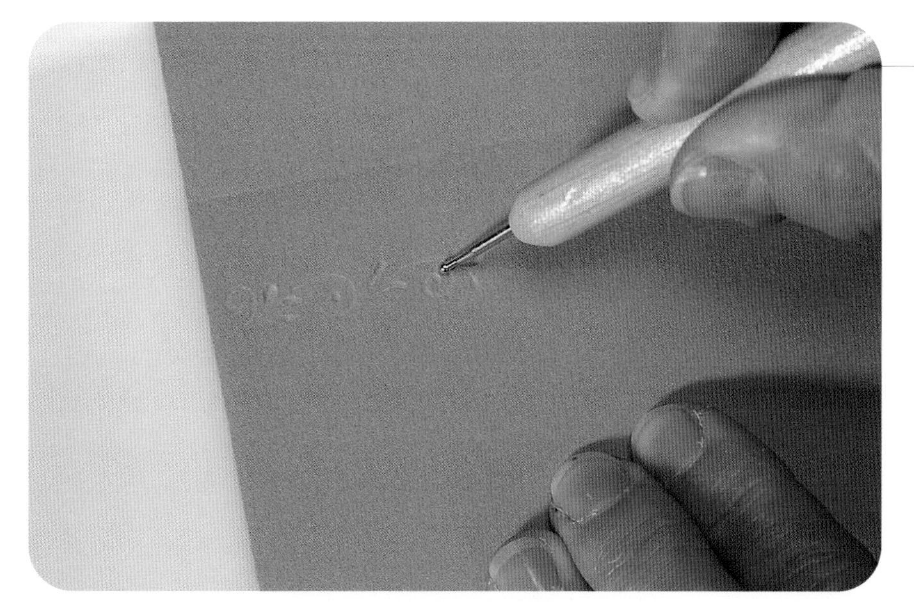

Emboss scroll on card 5

Attach the scroll pattern from the border stencil on the front of the card to make a vertical line down the left side. Flip stencil and card over onto light box and emboss.

Stencil scroll 6

Flip card to front and stencil the scroll pattern in Sap Green.

7 Finish embossing and stenciling

Repeat steps 5 and 6 until you have two or three vertical lines on both the left and right side of the card.

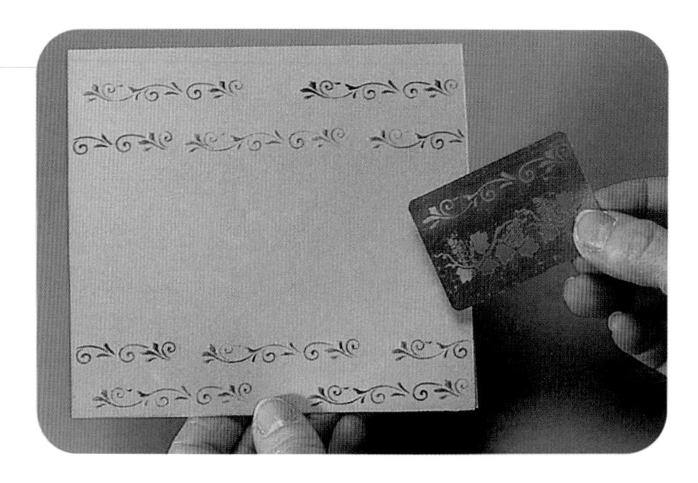

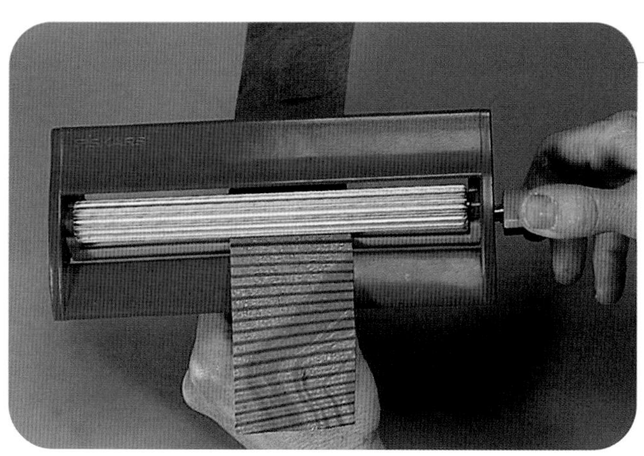

Cut and crimp green paper 8

Measure the unstenciled area down the center of the card. Trim the green paper to a width that will fit the crimper opening and run it through the paper crimper. If you don't have a paper crimper, you can accordion-fold the paper by hand or leave it uncrimped.

9 Cut and crimp beige accent strips

Run a piece of beige paper through the crimper and cut two ¼-inch-wide strips to approximately 2 inches long. If you don't have a crimper, make tiny accordion folds by hand.

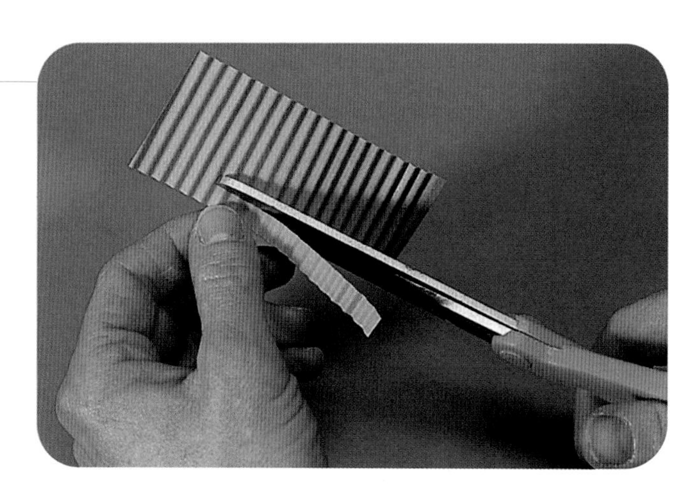

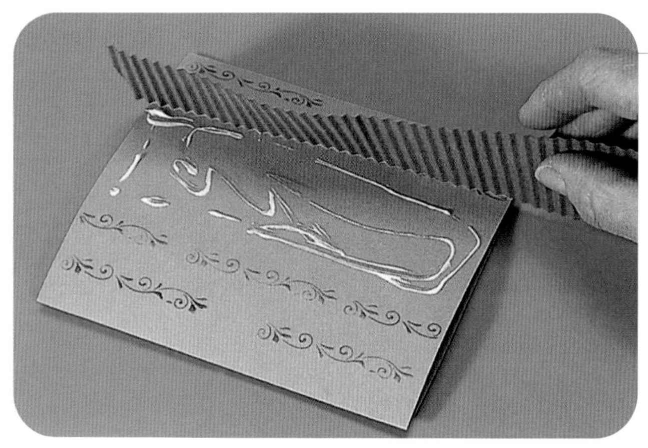

Attach green paper 10

Apply glue to the unstenciled portion of the front of the notecard. Affix the green crimped paper. Trim to fit.

11 Attach beige accent strips

Apply glue to the two beige strips of paper and affix them to the center of the card in the shape of an upside-down V. Touch on a little glue, then sprinkle glitter if desired.

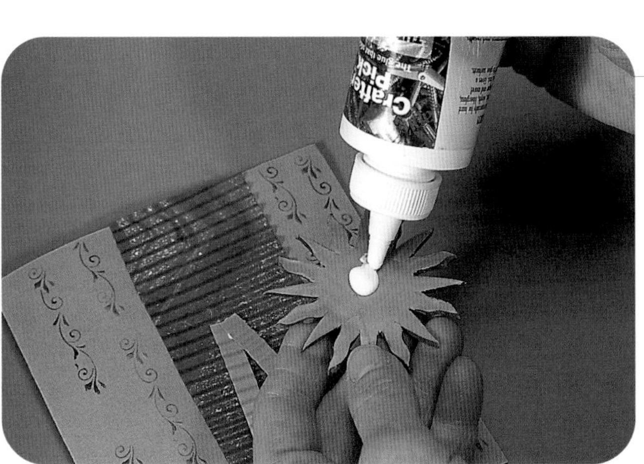

Attach the clay sun 12

Apply glue to the back of the dry clay sun. Center it on the card front just above where the beige strips are glued.

The finished card

Shrink Plastic Ornament Card

Shrink plastic is back and is being used for many craft projects, including rubber stamping and stenciling! Use shrink plastic in this chapter to make ornaments to hang from stenciled tree branches. If you decorate both sides of each ornament, the recipient can actually use them!

Materials

- American Traditional stencils
  - BL-79 Ornaments
  - BL-300 Ornaments 1
  - BL-301 Ornaments 2
  - BL-124 ⅜" Alphabet
  - FS-898 Merry Christmas (optional)
- Paper
  - 5½" x 4¼" white notecard with matching envelope
  - 8½"x 11" white cardstock
- 8" x 10" sheet of Aleene's Shrink-It or other shrink plastic
- Shiva Paintstiks
  - Azo Yellow
  - Naphthol Red
  - Ultramarine Blue
- DecoArt Americana acrylic paints
  - Hauser Dark Green
  - Yellow Light
  - Santa Red
- 3/16" stencil brushes
- scissors and craft knife
- masking tape
- pencil
- glue
- glitter in copper, green and silver or white
- heat gun
- fishing line
- Fiskars Scallop decorative edging scissors
- wax paper and foam plate

BL-300. To make a stencil, photocopy this image at 200 percent and use a sharp craft knife to cut out the design. (a)

BL-301. To make a stencil, photocopy this image at 200 percent and use a sharp craft knife to cut out the design. (b)

BL-79. To make a stencil, photocopy this image at 118 percent and use a sharp craft knife to cut out the design. (c)

BL-124. To make a stencil, photocopy this image at 100 percent and use a sharp craft knife to cut out the design. (d)

FS-898. To make a stencil, photocopy this image at 100 percent and use a sharp craft knife to cut out the design. (e)

(c)

(e)

Aa Bb Cc Dd Ee

Ff Gg Hh Ii Jj Kk

Ll Mm Nn Oo Pp

Qq Rr Ss Tt Uu

Vv Ww Xx Yy Zz

(d)

1 Trace tree on cardstock

Position tree from the stencil labeled Ornaments 1 on cardstock and trace with pencil. Do not trace the vertical cut line.

Cut new tree stencil 2

Cut out the entire tree. You have now created a new tree stencil. (You can keep the tree cutout for other projects.)

3 Stencil tree on plastic

Position the paper stencil on the shrink plastic and stencil it in Hauser Dark Green acrylic.

Cut out the plastic tree 4

Remove the paper stencil and cut the tree from the shrink plastic.

5 Add hole for hanging

Use a craft knife to cut a hole near the top of the tree. Make it large enough to allow for shrinkage.

Shrink the plastic 6

Hold the heat gun close to the tree to shrink it. The plastic will curl, but continue applying heat and it will flatten. You can use a chopstick or pencil to hold the piece as you are heating, if necessary.

7 Decorate tree

To decorate the tree, apply lines and dots of glue. Sprinkle glitter over the glue and shake off the excess. Apply the glue and glitter one color at a time.

Make more ornaments 8

Repeat steps 1 through 7 with the ornament shapes of your choice from Ornaments 1 and 2 stencils. Decorate with stenciling and glitter as desired. Thread 6 inches of fishing line through the hole at the top of an ornament and tie the ends in a knot.

9 Stencil lettering

Tape a piece of wax paper as a guide on the card front, about ½" from bottom. Stencil your message using green made from blue and yellow oil sticks. To center your lettering, find the middle letter and write it in the center of the card on the guide. Then fill in the rest. Or, center the "Merry Christmas" stencil on the card.

Stencil branches 10

Stencil the branches from the stencil labeled Ornaments on the front of the card using the green oil stick mixture made from blue and yellow.

Finish card

Trim the edge of the card with the decorative edging scissors. Drybrush a border on the inside card edge in green. Make small holes on the tree branches with a craft knife where you would like the ornaments to hang. Attach the ornaments to the tree branches by pushing the knots through the holes. Decorate your envelope to match the card.

Woodburned Teddy Postcard

Here's a unique project that creates not only a card, but a keepsake. If you back the wood veneer with stiff cardboard, this postcard will be strong enough to mail without an envelope. (Some veneers are strong enough without the backing.) Be sure to affix enough postage!

Materials

- American Traditional stencil BL-148 Floppy Bear
- 3 ½"x 5" piece of thin wood veneer
- 3"x 3" piece of clear Mylar
- craft knife
- scissors
- pencil
- fine-point black permanent marker
- colored pencils
- wood burner
- scrap paper
- stiff cardboard (optional)
- glue (optional)
- masking tape

BL-148. To make a stencil, photocopy this image at 65 percent and use a sharp craft knife to cut out the design. (a)

(You may also use the woodburner to cut the design out of Mylar.)

1 Cut veneer and trace stencil

Use scissors to cut the veneer to 3½" x 5". Tape stencil to veneer and trace design with a pencil.

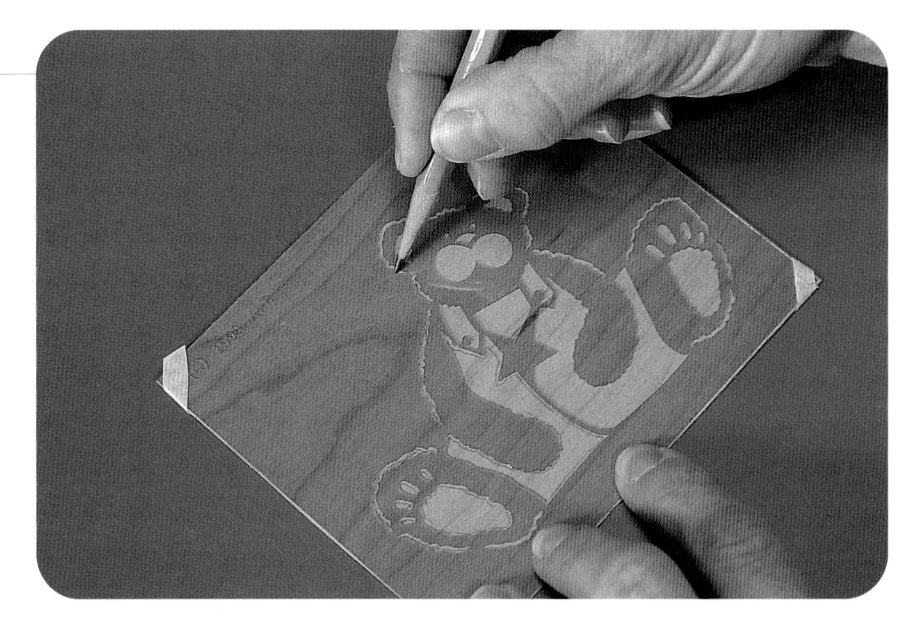

2 Burn design

Remove stencil. Trace over your pencil lines with the wood burner.

3 Add details

Use the tip of the wood burner to add little dots to represent fur and shading.

Create balloon stencil (4)

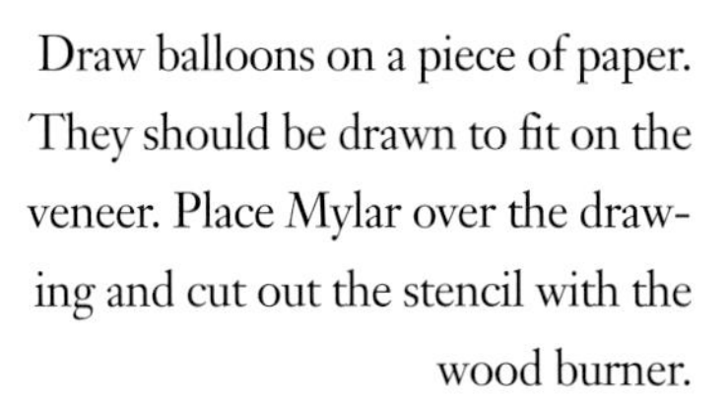

Draw balloons on a piece of paper. They should be drawn to fit on the veneer. Place Mylar over the drawing and cut out the stencil with the wood burner.

Trace balloon design (5)

Place the balloon stencil on the veneer and trace with a pencil. Remove the stencil.

Burn balloon design (6)

Trace over the pencil lines with the wood burner.

7 Add message

Write your message in pencil and then trace with the wood burner.

8 Singe edges

Use the inside of the wood burner to singe the outside edges of the postcard.

9 Add color

Color the teddy and balloons with colored pencils.

Detail with marker 10

Use a fine-point black permanent marker to add any finishing touches to the colored design.

Finish card

If the veneer is thick and strong, it can be mailed as is. If not, adhere a piece of stiff cardboard to the back with regular white glue. This will give you more room for a longer message. You can also enclose the postcard in an envelope to protect it.

RESOURCES

Stencils

You can purchase American Traditional stencils in quality art and craft supply stores worldwide. To purchase through mail order, contact

American Traditional Stencils
442 First New Hampshire Turnpike
Northwood, NH 03261-3401
(603) 942-8100
www.AmericanTraditional.com
or

The Stencil Outlet
P.O. Box 287
Northwood, NH 03261-0287
(603) 942-9957
Fax: (603) 942-8919

Organizations

For more information on stenciling, contact

Stencil Artisans League, Inc.
526 King St., Suite 423
Alexandria, VA 22314-3143
(703) 518-4375
Fax: (703) 706-9583
SALI@alexandriagroup.com
http://www.sali.org

Tools and Materials

Here's a list to help you find the tools and materials used in the projects in this book. Try your local craft store first; if you can't find it, you can always look here.

Glue and Shrink Plastic

Aleene's, Division of Artis, Inc.
85 Industrial Way
Buellton, CA 93427-9563
www.aleenes.com

Stencils, Brushes, Oil Sticks, Light Table, Embossing Tool and Cardstock

American Traditional Stencils
442 First NH Turnpike
Northwood, NH 03261-3401
www.AmericanTraditional.com

Mounting Memories Keepsake Glue

Beacon Adhesives/Signature Crafts
301 Wagaraw Rd.
Hawthorne, NJ 07506
www.beacon1.com

Pigment Inks

ColorBox by Clearsnap, Inc.
P.O. Box 98
Anacortes, WA 98221-0098
www.clearsnap.com

Shiva Paintstiks

Creative Art Products
P. O. Box 129
Knoxville, IL 61448

Acrylic Paints

DecoArt
P.O. Box 386
Stanford, KY 40484-0360
www.decoart.com

Duncan Enterprises
5673 East Shields Ave.
Fresno, CA 93727
www.duncancrafts.com

Zig 2-Way Glue and Markers

EK Success, Ltd.
611 Industrial Rd.
Carlstadt, NJ 07072-6507
www.eksuccess.com

Decorative Edge Scissors and Paper Crimper

Fiskars, Inc.
7811 W. Stewart Ave.
Wausau, WI 54401-9328
www.fiskars.com

Paper

Paper Adventures
P.O. Box 04393
Milwaukee, WI 53204-0361
www.introl.com/paperadv

Premo! Sculpey Polymer Clay

Polyform Products Co.
1901 Estes Ave.
Elk Grove Village, IL 60007-5415
www.sculpey.com

Embossing Powders and Heat Gun

Ranger Industries
15 Park Rd.
Tinton Falls, NJ 07724

Cray-pas Oil Pastels

Sakura of America
30780 San Clemente St.
Hayward, CA 94544-7131
www.gellyroll.com

Pigment Inks

Tsukineko, Inc.
15411 NE 95th St.
Redmond, WA 98052-2548
www.tsukineko.com

Ribbons

Wrights
85 South St., P.O. Box 398
West Warren, MA 01092-0398
www.wrights.com

Publications

Stencils, rubber stamps, and scrapbook memory pages all complement one another. Here is a list of magazines and books that are full of great ideas for cards!

The Rubber Stamper

Hobby Publications, Inc.,
225 Gordons Corner Rd.
P.O. Box 420
Englishtown, NJ 07726-0420

Somerset Studio/Stampington & Company
22992 Mill Creek, Suite B
Laguna Hills, CA 92653
(714) 380-7318

Making Great Scrapbook Pages
Published by Hot Off the Press

More Than Memories II
by Julie Stephani

Photo Keepsakes
by Suzanne McNeill

Creative Rubber Stamping Techniques
by MaryJo McGraw

Making Greeting Cards With Rubber Stamps
by MaryJo McGraw

INDEX